CHARLEY LAUREL

A STORY OF ADVENTURE BY SEA AND LAND

W. H. G. KINGSTON

1st WORLD
LIBRARY
Literary Society

Charley Laurel

W. H. G. Kingston

© 1st World Library, 2007
PO Box 2211
Fairfield, IA 52556
www.1stworldlibrary.com
First Edition

LCCN: 2007930909

Softcover ISBN: 978-1-4218-4868-6
Hardcover ISBN: 978-1-4218-4771-9
eBook ISBN: 978-1-4218-4965-2

Purchase *"Charley Laurel"*
as a traditional bound book at:
www.1stWorldLibrary.com/purchase.asp?ISBN=978-1-4218-4868-6

1st World Library is a literary, educational organization
dedicated to:

- Creating a free internet library of downloadable ebooks

- Hosting writing competitions and offering book publishing
scholarships.

Interested in more 1st World Library books? contact:
literacy@1stworldlibrary.com
Check us out at: www.1stworldlibrary.com

1ˢᵗ World Library Literary Society

Giving Back to the World

"If you want to work on the core problem, it's early school literacy."

- James Barksdale, former CEO of Netscape

"No skill is more crucial to the future of a child, or to a democratic and prosperous society, than literacy."

- Los Angeles Times

"Literacy... means far more than learning how to read and write... The aim is to transmit... knowledge and promote social participation."

- UNESCO

"Literacy is not a luxury, it is a right and a responsibility. If our world is to meet the challenges of the twenty-first century we must harness the energy and creativity of all our citizens."

- President Bill Clinton

"Parents should be encouraged to read to their children, and teachers should be equipped with all available techniques for teaching literacy, so the varying needs and capacities of individual kids can be taken into account."

- Hugh Mackay

CHAPTER ONE

VALUABLE BOOTY

A good many years ago, before, indeed, I can remember, His Majesty's Ship *Laurel*, a corvette of eighteen guns and a hundred and thirty men, commanded by Captain Blunt, formed one of the West India squadron.

She, with another corvette, and a brig in company, came one fine morning off a beautiful island, then in possession of the French, although, as Dick Driver, from whom I got the particulars, said, properly belonged to England, at least, it once had. Of course, therefore, it was their business to get it back again. Dick could not recollect its name, nor the exact date of the occurrences I am describing, for, being no scholar, he was a very bad hand at recollecting dates; and as he could not write his own name, of course it was not to be expected that he would keep a journal, or remember very accurately all the places he had visited.

The *Laurel* and her consorts, having hoisted French colours, stood along the coast, which the captain and officers of the former ship narrowly examined with their glasses.

At length the shades of evening drew on, and they came off a small town, situated on the shore of a bay, the entrance of which was guarded by a fort. The *Laurel* stood on, as if about to enter the bay, but the land-wind coming off the shore, she and the other two vessels stood away till they had got such a distance from the harbour that there was no chance of their being seen by the sharpest eyes, with the best of night-glasses, looking out for them.

The ships having hove-to, the commanders of the other vessels came on board the *Laurel*, when Captain Blunt announced his intention of attacking the town, hoping to hold possession of it till another squadron, which had been destined for the purpose, had captured a more important place on the other side of the island. The captain's plan was to send in the different boats of the squadron with a strong party of marines and blue-jackets, in three divisions, a couple of hours before daylight, as it was hoped at that time, the garrison of the fort being less on the alert than at an earlier hour, the boats might enter the bay unperceived.

The first and largest division was instructed to take possession of the town; the second was to attack the fort; and the third to cut out any vessels found in the harbour, in case the other two should be compelled to retreat, so that, at all events, there might be something to show for the night's work.

The boats' crews, and all who were fortunate enough, as they considered it, to be selected for the expedition, were soon busily employed in sharpening cutlasses, fitting fresh flints to their pistols, and making other preparations for the possible bloody work in which they were to be engaged. Dick Driver, who belonged to the cutter's crew, was among the most active. Dick was a short, strongly built, powerful fellow, with a broad, honest countenance, bright blue eyes, and fair bushy beard and whiskers,—a truer-hearted, braver seaman than Dick Driver never stepped.

"If this here cutlass of mine does its duty, we'll thrash the Mounseers, and gain the King his own again," exclaimed Dick, as he applied his weapon to the grindstone, feeling that he was a host in himself; and so he was, provided no treacherous bullet found its way through his sturdy frame, when, alas, Dick's strength and courage would have availed him nothing.

The boats at length collected round the *Laurel*; the oars were muffled; the officers were ordered to maintain a strict silence. It was hoped that by getting in the rear of the fort it might be taken with a rush, while the larger party entered the town, and took by surprise any troops who might be stationed within it.

The night was very dark, for clouds were in the sky, and the water was smooth.

The first lieutenant of the *Laurel*, who commanded the expedition, leading in the gig, away the boats pulled, keeping close together, and looking as they glided along like some huge serpent creeping on his prey. The entrance to the bay was gained without the boats being discovered. They dashed on more rapidly than before. In a few minutes they would be hard at work, the seamen slashing away with their cutlasses, and the marines firing, and pronging with their muskets and bayonets at their fellow-creatures.

Strange that men should like such work. Dick confessed he did, though he could not exactly say why.

The officers did their duty admirably; the marines were landed, and the blue-jackets were springing on shore before a shot was fired from the town.

Dick, who belonged to the first division, pushed on in that

direction with his party, while the other two attended to their destined duty. The gates of the fort, however, being closed, the intended rush could not be accomplished; and it was evident from the rapid firing that some hot work was going on there. Instead also of at once entering the town, the first party found their progress impeded by a somewhat numerous body of troops, who, quartered near at hand, turned out in time to defend it. The Frenchmen fought well, Dick acknowledged, though some had neither boots nor coats on, and many were destitute of other garments. They were, however, driven back inch by inch, till some turned tail and fled; the rest soon afterwards doing the same, followed by the victors, who fired indiscriminately at every one they saw in front of them. On such an occasion many of the unfortunate inhabitants were too likely to suffer, and many who had no arms in their hands, or had thrown them down and cried out for quarter, were shot before the officers could halt their men.

Meeting with two streets forking in different directions, some in the darkness had followed one and some the other. Flames were seen also bursting in the rear from houses set on fire either intentionally or by accident; while shouts and shrieks and cries arose in all directions. Altogether, the little town, which a few minutes before had been slumbering peacefully, was now the scene of havoc, terror, and confusion.

As Dick, cutlass in hand, was making his way along the dark street, a piteous cry reached his ears, and looking down, he saw lying wounded on the ground a black woman, holding up to him a little white child.

"Oh, save him! save him! or he will be killed!" she exclaimed.

"Of course I will," answered Dick, tucking the child under

his left arm; "and I'll help you into a house, where you may be safe."

He was about to perform the humane act he proposed, when there was a cry, "The French are coming on in force—fall back, men! fall back!"

Dick had only time to draw the poor woman on one side, when he was compelled, with his companions, rapidly to re-trace his steps. Not knowing where to deposit the child in safety, he kept it under his arm; and though on most occasions he would have been in the rank nearest the foe, he now, according to orders, retreated as fast as he could. Many of the other men had bundles of things they had picked up, but they were certainly not little children.

The boats were reached at last, though not until a good many of the gallant jollies and several of the blue-jackets had been shot down by a large body of French troops, who had come in from the farther side of the town. They were again, however, driven back far enough to allow the marines and sailors to embark.

Dick, unhurt, had reached the barge, still carrying his burden, for he had not the heart to throw it down, and could not find any safe place to put it in.

The fort had not been taken, but five merchantmen were captured and towed out of the harbour, in spite of the hot fire through which they had to pass.

Captain Blunt was very angry on finding that the men had brought away plunder from the town; and they were ordered to deliver it up, that it might be sent back to the inhabitants, whom, as he said, he had no intention of injuring.

Dick Driver, who among others had been seen to come aboard with a bundle, was ordered aft.

"Please, sir," said Dick, as he presented himself, holding a fine child in his arms of about four years old, "it ain't any booty, but a lawful gift. I was axed to take care of it, and I promised I would, and so I have."

"I do believe it's a little girl," exclaimed the captain, examining the delicate features and somewhat feminine appearance of the child, which had long fair locks hanging down over its shoulders.

"Lord bless you, no, sir! If it had been a she I shouldn't have known what to do with her—but it's as fine a youngster as I ever set eyes upon, barring his curls: and we will soon dock them, seeing they will be in his way, and not suited for the smart little tarpaulin I am going to make for him."

"What, my man, you don't expect to keep the child?" exclaimed the captain. "We must send him on shore with the rest of the property brought away."

"But, sir, he was given to me to look after by his dying mother," exclaimed Dick, forgetting for the moment that the child was white, and that the woman who had given it to him was as black as his shoe. "He is not like the rest of the booty, and if I may make so bold, I would like to keep him, and bring him up as one of the ship's company. We are all agreed that we will take precious good care of him, and he will be a greater favourite among us than either Quacho, or Jocko, or the old goat that went overboard in the last gale, or the pig as was killed when we were short of fresh provisions. Do, sir, let us keep him? We wouldn't part with the little chap for all the prize-money we have made this cruise."

Dick, in his anxiety to keep the child, had become desperate, and spoke with greater freedom than he would otherwise have ventured to do when addressing his captain. "If he were to be sent ashore there's no one might own him," he continued; "then what would become of the poor little chap? he might be taken to the workhouse, or just brought up nohow."

The captain, however, was not to be moved by all Dick's arguments.

"You did very rightly, my man, in saving the child's life, and you deserve a reward," he observed; "but we cannot turn the ship into a nursery, and he must run his chance of finding his friends. However, as you seem to have made a good nurse, you may take charge of him till we can send him away."

"Thank you, sir," said Dick, as he touched his hat, glad of even this short respite, and hoping that something might turn up to induce the captain to allow the child to remain on board. "We will take good care of him—that we will; and if he has to go back to his friends, we will see that he is in proper trim, so that they won't be nohow ashamed of him."

Dick, having thus delivered himself, swung his body round and hurried forward with light step, holding his young charge in his arms.

The *Laurel* and the other ships, with their prizes, were at this time standing away from the land. The seamen grumbled not a little at having to give up their booty: they could not understand why the merchantmen should have been cut out, and they not allowed to keep what they had picked up on shore.

An officer, who spoke French, now came from one of the

prizes with some important information which he had obtained from a prisoner. It was to the effect that three heavy French frigates were hourly expected off the coast. Captain Blunt accordingly ordered a bright look-out to be kept for any strange sail. In a short time three were descried standing along shore. There could be no doubt that they were the enemy's frigates; and as the two corvettes and brig could not hope to cope with them, all sail was made to escape. The enemy soon afterwards were seen crowding all sail in chase: the prizes were ordered by signal to separate and to make the best of their way to Jamaica, while the *Laurel* and her consorts stood to the eastward, under all the canvas they could spread. Before nightfall they had run their powerful foes out of sight.

The next day a heavy gale sprang up, which increased to a hurricane. A signal of distress was made by the unfortunate ten-gun brig, while the other sloop was evidently in a bad plight.

During the night, the *Laurel* having to run before the gale, lost sight of both of them. The gale continuing longer than usual, ere it ceased she found herself in a the wide waters of the Atlantic, with all her boats washed away or stove in, her three top-masts gone, and besides other damages, a leak sprung, which kept the pumps going for the best part of each watch.

W. H. G. Kingston

CHAPTER TWO

THE LIFE-RAFT

The *Laurel* had for some days been becalmed, and though every one on board, from the captain to the smallest powder-monkey, had been whistling for a breeze to carry her back to look after her prizes and consorts, no breeze came.

Dick had been the busiest of the busy. He now appeared, with no small pride in his countenance, leading by the hand a little boy dressed in a seaman's jacket and trowsers, his shirt-collar turned down, and a little tarpaulin hat stuck on the top of his curly head. He went boldly aft, till he reached the captain, who, with several officers, was standing on the quarterdeck.

"Touch your hat, Charley," said Dick. Charley obeyed promptly with a true sailor's manner, showing that his guardian had, according to his own ideas, commenced his education, and had at all events taught him to be obedient.

"Please, sir, this here little chap is Charley Laurel, as I brought aboard t'other night," began Dick. "Some wanted to call him one name, some another. We called him Charley, sir, after Mr Slings, the boatswain, who offered to stand godfather; and 'cause, as I may say, he belongs to all of us, we have given him the name of Laurel, after the old barky, if that's agreeable to you, sir."

"I have no objection to any name you may give him," answered the captain; "but I warn you that we shall have before many weeks to restore him to his friends, when we shall find out his proper one, and I have no doubt they will be glad to reward you for the care you have taken of him."

"I want no reward, sir, except perhaps a glass of grog to drink their healths, and small thanks we will give them if they take him from us. It will be hard to lose him as well as our other booty, especially when he takes to us so kindly. To my mind, he will be much better off with us than among them niggers, who will just spoil him with sugar-cane and letting him have his own way. Besides, sir, the black woman gave him to me, and unless you says so, we will not hand him over to them."

Dick slapped his leg as he spoke, as a clencher to his assertion, and in his eagerness was going to use a strong expression, when, recollecting that he was on the quarterdeck, and to whom he was speaking, he stopped short.

"Well, my man," said the captain, good-naturedly, not offended with Dick's freedom, "make the most of the little fellow while you have him, and we will see what to do with him by-and-by."

There is an old saying which should never be forgotten, that "Man proposes, but God disposes."

It was the hurricane season. Captain Blunt had been doing his best to get the damages the ship had received repaired. He was pacing the deck, and every now and then casting an anxious eye round the horizon, knowing well that the gallant little *Laurel* was ill able to withstand either a gale or an enemy, by either of which she might be assailed, although, like a true sailor, he was ready to meet the one or the other with undaunted courage.

The ocean was like a sheet of glass, and the hot sun struck down on the deck with tremendous force. Those who could, sat in the shade, those who could not, as Dick observed, "had to grin and bear it, though it was not much odds where a man got to, it was hot everywhere."

Now and then a covey of flying-fish might be seen skimming over the ocean, but they came out of the water to avoid the jaws of their persevering foes, the dolphins or bonitos, not because they liked it, or wished to exhibit their brilliant wings, but the wiser leviathans of the deep kept in the cooler regions below the surface. Gradually a thin mist filled the atmosphere; it seemed to come from nowhere, but there it was, though the heat was in no way diminished by it, but rather increased. Still the pumps had to be kept going, and the crew had to stand at them, whether in sunshine or shade, stripped to the waist, the perspiration running down from every pore. No one grumbled, though "spell ho!" was oftener than usual cried, and numerous visits were paid to the water-cask by those who generally disdained the pure liquid unless mixed with rum.

The captain's countenance wore an unwonted grave expression; the officers, too, looked serious, and their eyes were constantly turned round, now in one direction, now in the other. Presently the captain shouted with startling energy—

"All hands shorten sail! clew up! haul down! Be smart, my lads!"

The courses were quickly brailed up and furled, the

fore-staysail alone being set. A dark cloud was seen away to the south-west, gathering as it approached a vast assemblage of black masses which appeared to come out of space, advancing rapidly till they formed one dense column.

The men were scarcely off the yards when a sheet of white foam came hissing over the hitherto calm surface of the ocean, followed by a deafening roar as wave after wave arose, each higher than its predecessor, and then the hurricane in all its irresistible might struck the sorely-battered ship. Over she heeled before it, the fore-staysail with a loud report flew out of the bolt-ropes ere it had done its duty of paying off the ship's head. Again and again the savage blast struck her side, pressing her still farther down, while the ever-increasing seas broke in foaming masses over her. The captain gave the order to cut away the mizzen-mast, and set another staysail. For a moment there was a lull, the ship rose, and her head feeling the wind, away she flew before the howling gale. The carpenter sounded the well. He had an alarming report to make to the captain—the water was gaining faster than ever on the ship. Dick heard it.

"To my mind the old barky will be going down," he said to himself. "I must look after Master Charley, for if she does, it won't do to have the little chap going to Davy Jones' locker. It is all very well for those as are bred to it, but, bless his young heart! I must do what I can to keep him afloat."

Dick was a man of action rather than words. He immediately filled his capacious pockets with all the provisions he could lay hands on. In the launch on deck he found a basket which had been brought on board with vegetables. There were a number of broken spars and other fragments of wood, the remains of the boats which had been carried away. He began to lash them firmly together in a mode which a seaman only could have accomplished; and in the centre of the raft he had

W. H. G. Kingston

thus formed he secured the basket, which had a lid to it. One of the officers saw him, and told him to knock off.

"Ay, ay!" he answered; but it was not a moment, he conceived, to stand on ceremony, and immediately again went on with his work. The boatswain also set his eyes on him.

"What are you about there, Dick?" he asked. "Off with you to the pumps; it will be your spell directly."

"I am building a raft for your godson, Mr Slings," answered Dick. "You would not wish the pretty little chap to be drowned if there's a chance of saving him, and please Heaven, I will try and do it, though I am as ready as any on myself to stick to the old barky to the last."

"Don't you be talking of the ship going down," exclaimed the boatswain, gruffly; "you will be making the rest chicken-hearted."

"You know as well as I do, Mr Slings, that go down she will, before many hours are over, unless old 'Harry Cane' takes himself off pretty smartly."

Dick could not resist the sailor's common joke even at that moment.

"I cannot say you nay, Dick," answered the boatswain; "but all this comes of having babies aboard; we must try and keep the ship above water, anyhow."

The raft being completed, Dick got hold of a small beaker of water, which he secured to it; he also formed a paddle, and laid alongside of it a spar of considerable length. Having finished his work, he slipped below, and brought up little

Charley, with a bundle of bedding and a blanket. The child greatly objected to go to bed in the basket, and still more so to be lashed in, as Dick was doing. Dick knew that nobody would interfere with the child, but still he placed him as much out of sight as possible, just abaft the fore-mast.

"You be good boy, Charley, and don't cry out," he said, trying to soothe him. "There is a biscuit—chaw it, lad. I have to take a spell at the pumps, and will be back directly."

As soon as Dick could leave his work at the pumps, he hurried back to the child, and threw himself down to rest by his side.

The ship flew on before the gale. Every one, knowing that their lives depended on their exertions, laboured away with desperation: some were sent below to bale with buckets, which were passed up to others stationed on deck, but all their efforts, it appeared too likely, would be of no avail. Still the water gained on them. The only hope was that the hurricane might cease, and that a sail might be got under the ship's bottom. Preparations were made for doing this as soon as it was practicable, but the wind blew harder and harder. The main-mast had before been badly sprung, and during one of the fearful lurches the ill-fated ship made, down it came, crushing the launch, on which depended the only hope of saving the lives of some of them. Dick rushed forward, fearing his little charge had suffered, but Charley still lay unhurt in his basket on the raft. Suddenly there came a lull, and the hurricane ceased almost as rapidly as it had commenced: the sea, however, still tumbled and tossed about fiercely on either side, the ship lying helpless in the midst of the foaming waves. The crew laboured as gallantly as before, though their stout arms were giving way, and many knew too well that all hope was nearly gone. Some with the sharpest eyes were sent to the mast-head, to look out for any

W. H. G. Kingston

ship which might have approached before the calm came on; but as they cast their anxious eyes around the horizon, not a sail was to be seen rising out of the dark tumbling waters.

Dick had gone again to the pumps. "Spell ho!" he cried, for he had worked till he could work no longer. He had just thrown himself down by the side of the raft when a fearful cry arose.

"The ship is sinking! the ship is sinking!"

Dick seated himself on the raft, with a spar in his hand which he had prepared. Lower and lower the gallant ship sank. Many of the crew were at the pumps; some were still below, some running to the forecastle, others aft. Dick kept his post. The water rushed in at the ports—the raft floated—a surge carried it overboard, Dick urging it by a shove which sent it far away from the ship's side.

The *Laurel* gave one plunge forward—her stern rose in the air—and down she glided beneath the tumultuous waters. One fearful shriek arose of strong men in their agony. Some few attempted to reach the raft, but they were drawn down in the vortex caused by the sinking ship. Dick vigorously plied his paddle, and though tumbled and tossed fearfully about, he got far enough off to escape the danger of being drawn down with the rest. Had he not had Charley to look after, he would have shared the fate of his shipmates, he thought; and so he would, I am sure. Though he was himself frequently under water, and often almost washed off the little raft, the child, protected in the basket, remained nearly dry. As Dick gazed back towards where the stout ship had lately floated, he could see a few struggling forms with arms outstretched, and hear their last cries for help ere they sank for aye, till that awful day when the sea shall give up its dead; and in a few minutes he and little Charley were the only living beings of all the gallant fellows who had formed the crew of the ill-fated *Laurel*.

W. H. G. Kingston

CHAPTER THREE

DICK'S PRAYER

Night had come and passed away since the gallant *Laurel* had sunk. The sea had much gone down, and Dick, no longer compelled to hold on for his life, was able to open the basket and give Charley, who was crying out for his breakfast, some food.

"Where de ship?" inquired Charley, in his imperfect English and little innocent fashion. "Where we got to? Why not give me hot tea? Why give me wet biscuit?"

"Don't ask questions, Charley," answered Dick. "If I have a fancy for taking a cruise on this here raft, you should be content—you know I have charge of you; and if I didn't think it the best thing to be done, I wouldn't have brought you here."

"All right," said Charley. "More biscuit, please. Now I sing song to you, Dick," and the little chap struck up the stave of a ditty which Dick had taught him, evidently feeling in no way alarmed at the fearful position in which he was placed.

"I think, Charley, you should say your prayers," said Dick, who had taught the boy those he had himself learned in his childhood. "Ask God to take care of you, Charley; for I am sure if He does not no one else will, either here or anywhere else. He hears your prayers as well as big people's, so don't be afraid of asking Him for what you want; and just now I have a notion we want Him to send a ship this way to pick us up."

Charley turned round, and kneeling up in his basket, lifted his small hands towards the blue sky, and asked the kind Father he believed dwelt there to take care of him and Dick, and send a ship to pick them up.

Dick gazed affectionately at the child as he prayed.

"That's done me good," he said to himself. "I am sure He who lives up there will do what that innocent little cherub asks. What He would say if a rough wild chap like me was to pray, is a different matter; and yet I mind that mother used to tell me He will hear any one who is sorry for what they have done amiss, and trust to His Son who died for sinners. But it's a hard matter to mind all the bad things a man like me has done, and I hope He ain't so over particular with respect to poor sailors."

Dick at length, mustering courage, knelt by the side of the child, the calm sea allowing him to do so without the danger of falling off. His prayer might not have been, as he expressed it, very ship-shape; the chief expression in it was, "Lord be merciful to me a sinner, and take care of little Charley here and me, if such a one as I am is worth looking after."

At length Dick resumed his seat by the side of his charge. The sun came down with intense heat, but he managed, by turning the raft round with his paddle, and lifting the lid of the basket, to shelter Charley from its burning rays. The child sat up and looked about him, prattling away frequently in a lingo Dick could not understand: sometimes also he spoke a little English, which he seemed to have known before he came on board the *Laurel*, but since then he had picked up a good many words. Dick now tried to amuse him and himself by teaching him more, and as the child learned rapidly whatever he heard, he already could sing—

"Cease, rude Boreas, blustering railer,
List ye landsmen all to me."

and—

"One night it blew a hurricane,
The sea was mountains rolling,
When Barney Buntline turned his quid,
And cried to Billy Bowlin—"

right through without a mistake.

"Oh, look dere, dere! what dat rum fis?" he suddenly exclaimed, pointing to a short distance from the raft.

Dick looked, and saw what a sailor dreads more than any human foe—the black triangular fin of a huge shark which was noiselessly gliding by, just beneath the surface, and turning its wicked eye towards Charley and himself. A blow from the monster's tail or nose might easily upset the raft, when they to a certainty would become its prey. Dick grasped his pole to do battle, should the creature come nearer, and he at once began beating the water on every side and shouting at the top of his voice. The shark, an arrant coward by nature, kept at a distance, but his dark fin could still be seen as he circled round and round the raft, waiting, Dick feared, for an opportunity to rush in and make an attack.

"He shall pay for it with one of his eyes, if he does," said Dick to himself.

"What for make all that noise?" asked Charley.

"Why do you sing out 'youngster' sometimes?" inquired Dick. "Because you have a fancy for it, I've a notion, and so I have a fancy just now to shout away. I mus'n't frighten the little chap," he muttered to himself. "It won't do to tell him what Jack Shark is looking after."

Thus Dick sat on till he thought by the position of the sun that it must be noon, when he gave Charley his dinner and cup of water—he himself eating but sparingly, for fear of diminishing his scanty store and depriving the child of food.

"I can hold out much longer than he can," he said to himself, "and I must not let him get into bad case."

Every now and then Dick stood up and gazed around the horizon, anxiously looking out for the signs of a breeze which might bring up some ship. The sun was again sinking beneath the ocean, which continued glass-like as before. At length night crept over the world of waters, and the brilliant stars shone down from the dark sky, each one reflected clearly in the mirror-like deep.

"What all those pretty things up dere?" asked Charley, waking suddenly from his first sleep; "get me some to play wid, Dick."

"Just what I can't do, boy," answered Dick. "All those are stars far away in the sky, and I have heard say they are worlds; but how they stop up is more than I can tell, except God keeps them there."

"God do many things we can't," said Charley. "But if I ask Him, would He give me some to play wid?"

"No, Charley, He gives us what we want and what is good for us, but He chooses to keep those stars where they are, for He knows that if He sent one of them down they would only do us harm. Now, Charley, don't be asking more questions; just lie down and go to sleep again," and Dick shut down the lid of the basket.

Charley's questions, however, had set his mind at work, and as he gazed up in the sky he thought more than he had ever done before of those wondrous lights which he had always seen there, and yet had troubled himself so little about. And then he was led to think of the God who made them and governs their courses, and many things he had heard in his boyhood came back to his mind.

"Mother used to say He is a kind and loving God, and so I am sure He will take care of this little chap, and me, too, for his sake."

Dick at length felt very sleepy. He had been afraid to shut his eyes, for fear of the shark, but he could no longer prevent the drowsiness creeping over him: he lashed himself therefore to the raft, to escape the risk of falling off it, and placing his head on the basket, closed his weary eyelids.

The bright beams of the great red sun rising above the horizon as they fell on his eyes awoke him, and on looking round he caught sight of the fin of the shark gliding by a few feet off. The monster's eye was turned up towards him with a wicked leer, and he believed that in another instant the savage creature would have made a grab at the raft. His pole was brought into requisition, and the rapid blows he gave with it on the water soon made the monster keep at a respectful distance. He would not shout out, for fear of waking Charley.

The boy slept on for a couple of hours longer, and when he at length awoke, seemed none the worse for what he had gone through. Dick had cut up some little bits of meat and biscuit, that he might not have to wait for breakfast after he awoke. He had on the previous day carefully dried his clothes and bedding, and given him such food as he required—the child, indeed, could not have had a better nurse.

Dick calculated that the store of provisions he had stowed away in the basket and his own pockets would last a week, and he hoped before the termination of that time to be picked up. He, in reality, in consequence of anxiety, suffered more than the child: had he been alone, he probably would not have felt so much.

The day passed away as before. Occasionally sea-birds flew overhead, and huge fish were seen swimming by, or breaking the calm surface as they poked up their noses or leaped into the air.

"Oh, Dick, Dick, what dat?" suddenly exclaimed Charley. As he spoke, a dozen flying-fish, their wings glittering in the bright sun, leaped on to the raft, some tumbling into the child's basket.

Dick quickly secured them, for though unwilling to feed the little boy with raw fish, they would, he knew, afford him an ample meal or two. Charley, however, begged to have some to play with, and was much surprised to find their beautiful wings quickly become dry, and that in a few seconds they were dead.

W. H. G. Kingston

Dick enjoyed a better supper than he had had since the hurricane began, and he always afterwards declared that those fish had kept his body and soul, when he would otherwise have been starved—although those he reserved for a meal on the following day required a keen appetite to munch up.

Day after day Dick and his charge floated on the calm ocean. He was becoming weaker than he had ever before been in his life, and yet he would take but a few drops of water from the beaker, and would not eat a particle of the food more than was necessary to keep the life in him, so fearful was he of not having enough for Charley. Yet Dick had not been distinguished among his shipmates for any especial good qualities, except that he was looked upon as a good-natured, kind-hearted, jovial fellow, and brave as the bravest; yet so were many of the *Laurel's* gallant crew, now sleeping their last sleep beneath the ocean.

The faithful fellow now often found himself dropping off to sleep when he wished to be awake—and afraid that on one of these occasions Charley might get out of his basket and tumble overboard, to make such an accident impossible, he tied him down by the legs in such a way as to allow the child to sit up when inclined, and look about him.

Poor Dick, who was getting very weak, was lying down asleep with his head on the edge of the basket, when he heard Charley's voice sing out—

"See, see—what dat?"

Dick opened his eyes, and casting them in the direction the child pointed, caught sight of a large vessel under all sail running down before the wind, which she brought up with her.

"A ship, Charley, a ship!" cried Dick. "And we must do what we can to make her see us, or she may be passing by, and we shall be no better off than we are now."

He instantly took off his shirt, which he fastened by its sleeves to the pole. Holding it aloft as the ship drew near, with all his strength he waved it to and fro, shouting out in his anxiety, and not aware how low and hollow his voice sounded. Charley shouted too, with his childish treble, though their united voices could not have reached by a long way as far as the ship was from them. It seemed to Dick that she would pass at some distance: his heart sank. Presently his eye brightened.

"She has altered her course; she is standing this way," he cried out. "Charley, we shall be picked up!"

"Then I thank God—He hear my prayer. I ask ship come—ship do come," said Charley.

"You are right, boy—you are right!" cried Dick. "And I was forgetting all about that prayer of yours."

The tall ship glided rapidly over the ocean, the surface of which was now rippled with miniature wavelets as the freshening breeze swept across it.

"To my eye, she is a foreign ship of war," observed Dick. "But a friend in need is a friend indeed, and we may be thankful to be taken on board by her or any other craft. Even if a 'Mounseer' had offered to pick us up, I would not have refused."

The ship approaching was hove-to, a boat being lowered from her, which, with rapid strokes, pulled towards the raft.

W. H. G. Kingston

CHAPTER FOUR

THE PIRATE SHIP

Dick and the little boy were lifted off the raft, with the basket and cask, and placed in the stern of the boat. The crew were swarthy fellows with red caps, and Dick at once saw that the uniform worn by the officers in command was neither English nor French. They appeared to be talking gibberish, but such indeed were all foreign languages to him. He asked Charley if it was the French lingo.

"Not know what they say," answered Charley.

"I suppose, however, that they will give us something to eat and drink," observed Dick. "And so, whoever they may be, we shall be better off than on the raft."

On getting alongside, Dick was hoisted on board, and one of the men carried Charley up in his arms.

Numerous questions were at once put to Dick, every one seeming anxious to know how he and the boy came to be on the raft. He replied by pointing to his lips, and showing by other signs that he was hungry and thirsty. When it was discovered that he was either too weak to speak, or that he did not understand their language, he was carried below and placed in a hammock, while the officers took charge of little Charley, who was soon at home among them. A rough-looking fellow brought Dick a mess of some sort in basin, and a horn cup filled with stiff grog. A sailor seldom refuses a glass of grog, and although water was what he then wanted, he drank the spirit off, and ate some of the food. The effect of the grog was to send him into a sound sleep, from which he did not awake till the next day. He felt by that time pretty strong, and, turning out, went on deck. He found that he was on board a flush-decked ship-rigged vessel, heavily armed, with a numerous crew of dark-skinned savage-looking fellows, most of them wearing long knives or daggers in their belts. He thought that perhaps they might be Spaniards or Portuguese, then the idea occurred to him that they were Algerines or Salee rovers, of whom he had heard. However, seeing some of them with leaden crucifixes round their necks, he came to the conclusion that they were Spaniards. Not one of them could speak a word of English, and Dick was ignorant of every language except his own.

The ship lying becalmed, the crew seemed to take it very easily, some sitting down between the guns, amusing themselves with cards or dice, while others were asleep on the deck. Going aft, and looking down the skylight, which was open, Dick saw that the officers were employed much as their men, only they were gambling with large gold pieces as stakes.

"These may be honest gentlemen, or may be not," he thought to himself. "However, if they are kind to Charley, I don't mind what they are, and I suppose for his sake they won't make me walk the plank. I wonder where the little chap can be," and he looked down the companion-hatch, though he did not venture to descend.

The officer of the watch seemed to understand what he

W. H. G. Kingston

wanted, and going to the head of the companion-ladder, shouted out, "Pedro!" and some other words, and presently a black man appeared with Charley in his arms, and handed him over to Dick.

"Much obliged to you, friend," said Dick; "he is a fine little chap, isn't he?"

The black grinned and seemed to understand him, and patted the child on the head.

"Well, Charley, my boy, have they treated you well?" asked Dick, as he took up the child and kissed him affectionately.

Charley said that the gentlemen had been kind, and had given him all sorts of things to eat, and some strong stuff to drink, which made him sleep most of the time.

Dick carried Charley to the only shady spot he could find unoccupied, and sat down with him on his knees. Charley prattled away merrily, but he soon stopped and complained of a headache, and of the strong stuff the officers had given him to drink. This made Dick suspect that they had been amusing themselves by trying to make the child tipsy.

"It was a shame in them," exclaimed Dick, indignantly. "You must stay by me, Charley. I can't trust you out of my sight."

Dick after this kept Charley by his side, and at night made him sleep in his hammock.

Several days passed by, and the ship lay without movement on the smooth ocean. A breeze at length springing up, the crew were all life and activity, with a look-out at each mast-head. Towards noon a sail was espied, and all sail was made in chase. She was a brig under English colours. On the stranger being come up with, a gun was fired across her bows; and as she did not heave-to, a shot was sent crashing into her hull. She then hauled down her colours. The boats were manned and shoved off to her. They quickly returned, laden almost to the water's edge. The ship stood on again nearer to her, when the boats towed her alongside. Her cargo, consisting of bales of merchandise, was transferred to the ship.

"I thought so," said Dick, when he saw the proceedings. "She is no better than she should be, and if it had not been for this little chap, I would rather have remained on the raft than have come aboard her. I wonder what they will do with the crew."

That matter was soon, to Dick's horror, settled. One after the other he saw the poor fellows compelled to walk to the end of a long plank, when the inner end was lifted up and they were sent overboard. The brig was set on fire, and the pirate, letting down the sheets, proceeded on her course.

Some days after this, when Dick came on deck, he saw at a short distance a small island with a few cocoa-nut trees growing on it. Several of the officers who were on deck were consulting together, every now and then casting a look at him and Charley. At last one of them called him up and made him understand that they were well-disposed towards him, and that as they understood he had been the means of saving the life of the little child, they wished to treat him kindly—that otherwise he would have shared the fate of the brig's crew, if they had not left him on the raft to perish. To show their regard, they intended to land him on the island, where he would find water and sufficient food to support life; though, if he wished it, they would take care of the child, to follow their noble profession.

"Thank you for nothing," answered Dick. "I would sooner heave the little chap overboard, to be munched up by a shark, than leave him with you; and as to quitting the ship without him, I will not do it; but if it please you to put him and me on shore, I'll go willingly enough, and trust to One better able to take care of us than you are."

Though the pirates did not understand what Dick said, they comprehended that he was perfectly willing to be left on the island. A boat was accordingly lowered, and numerous articles which the pirates had taken out of the brig, and were likely to prove useful to him, were put into her. Charley ran up and shook hands with the officers, but hastened back immediately to Dick, for he was afraid of being left behind. Poor little fellow, he felt grateful to them for their kindness, having no notion of the villains they were.

Dick, taking him in one arm, descended the ship's side into the boat, which pulled away towards the land. Numerous shoals and rocks surrounded the island, among which the boat threaded her way, and at length landed him and the boy, with the articles they had brought, on the sandy beach of a sheltered bay.

Dick had no inclination to shake hands with the crew who had so lately murdered his countrymen, and probably very many people besides, nor did he feel at his ease till he saw the boat again pulling out towards the ship. As soon as she had gone, Dick, who had held Charley in his arms, placed him on a rock, and examined the articles which had been sent with him.

"I am much obliged to the villains, at all events," he said; "but can only wish them a better calling and a happier end than most of them are likely to meet with. To be sure, they can afford to be generous, seeing that they stole the things and had more than they could use. Here are some carpenter's tools, a saw and axe, a hammer and nails, and a piece of canvas that will do for a tent; a bale of cloth, and calico, and needles, and thread; here are fish-hooks and lines, and shoes; three casks of flour and rice, and some pots, and pans, and knives; and a decent-looking fowling-piece and powder and shot. Well, if I hadn't seen what I did see, I should have taken them to be kind-hearted decent chaps, who, for some reason or other, didn't wish to keep me among them, and so had put me ashore, and wished to do their best to make me comfortable. Ah, I have a notion how it is—the skipper, or one or other of them has got a little chap like this at home, and they have done it for his sake; and savage as their hearts may be, they didn't quite like keeping him on board their wicked-doing craft. Yes, that's it; so if I have saved Charley's life, he has saved mine, though he doesn't know it, bless him!"

Dick having finished his soliloquy, cut a pole from a tree growing near, and quickly rigged up a tent, beneath which he placed Charley out of the heat of the sun. He then collected wood, of which there was an abundance on the beach, and soon had a fire burning, and next proceeded to cook some of the provisions for Charley and himself. Not far off was a spring of water, which would afford him an abundant supply of that necessary of life.

"We sha'n't be so badly off, Charley, after all," he said; "only I hope these fellows won't come back again, in case they may take it into their heads to carry you away."

"I will not leave you, Dick," answered the boy, taking his hand and beginning to cry at the thought.

"You sha'n't, Charley, you sha'n't," said Dick. "We will move away to another part of the island, where they cannot find us;

may be there is water elsewhere, that's what we shall want most. There are plenty of cocoa-nuts, and I dare say other vegetables, and with the gun I shall be able to shoot birds, and with the hooks catch as many fish as we shall want. We are better off than on the raft, anyhow."

Dick having made up a bed with the cloth for Charley to sleep on, cut some grass for himself, and then prepared to pass the night.

"You say your prayers, Charley," said Dick; "and mind you thank God for bringing us ashore in safety."

Dick had a feeling that the little innocent boy could offer up his prayers more effectually than he himself could; but yet Dick did his best to pray in his own fashion, though he could seldom say more than, "I am a desperately wicked fellow; God be merciful to me, and, if He thinks fit, take care of me and make me better."

He, however, taught Charley a much longer prayer than this, suitable, as he considered, to his condition.

The rough sailor and the child having finished their devotions, lay down on their beds, and, fearless of evil, fell asleep.

Next day after breakfast Dick, leading Charley by one hand and taking his gun in the other, set out to explore the island. On reaching the top of the nearest height, which was of no great elevation, being a mass of barren rock thrown up by some convulsion of nature, he looked around him. The island was of small size, a couple of miles perhaps in length and about a quarter as broad, with deep indentations, bays, or small gulfs. The larger portion was barren, but here and there were spots overgrown with the richest vegetation of the tropics. The shores were rocky, but in no part high, while around in every direction were seen extensive reefs, some rising above the water, others only to be distinguished by the line of foam which danced above them.

"From the look of the place, ships are likely to give this a wide berth," observed Dick. "However, we can manage to live here pretty comfortably, and may be some day or other we shall get off again, but how, is more than I can tell."

On descending from the hill they reached a cocoa-nut grove. Dick looked up at the nuts, now almost ripe, with a well-satisfied eye.

"We will have some of those before long, and the milk will be good food for you, Charley," he observed. "Ah, and we shall have some cabbages, too." He pointed to some smaller palm-trees, the crown of which yields the cabbage, so prized in the tropics as one of the most delicious vegetables.

Sometimes Dick carried Charley on his shoulders, sometimes he let him run alongside him, and he thus made his progress to the farther end of the island. One part appeared very barren, low, and sandy, with wild rocks rising up on either side.

"After all, this place may be our best hunting-ground," observed Dick, on discovering that it was the habitation of wild fowl, who came there to lay their eggs and rear their young.

At length he reached the extreme end of the island. Near it was a grove of cocoa-nut and other palms, a beautiful sandy bay, and what Dick was in search of, a spring of clear water which bubbled out of the rock.

"We shall be better off here, and out of the way of those

W. H. G. Kingston

gentry if they return to the island, and I don't think they will come so far to look for us," said Dick. "We will move up the stores, and after that I will build a hut; it will be more comfortable than the tent, especially in the hurricane season, and we can't tell how long we may have to stop."

Dick having discovered that, by keeping partly inland and partly near the shore, a tolerably easy road existed from one end of the island to the other, he built a little hand-dray, in which, he conveyed the stores to the new location. It occupied several days, but, as he said, time being their own, he had no need to be in a hurry. He next put up a hut, for which the trees growing around and the planking from some unfortunate vessel dashed to pieces on the reefs afforded abundance of material, while the palm-leaves served for a thatch. He could not also be long content without a boat. Though not an expert ship-builder, he managed to knock together a contrivance in which he could venture out within the reefs in calm weather to fish with Charley.

"We live like princes, my boy," he said, "but I wish some-how I was able to look after your education; though if we had books I could not make use of them, seeing I never learned to read."

Charley replied that he was very happy without books, and he supposed when he grew up to be a big boy he should find the means of learning.

"I don't know when that may be, though," observed Dick. "We have been here now some months, and I have never yet caught sight of a sail. However, though I cannot give you learning, I can teach you religion, and I will try and recollect all I ever knew. I can remember the ten commandments, or most of them, which I learned at school, and they will do to begin with, and as we go on, may be I shall brush up more."

Dick was as good as his word, and at night frequently lay awake trying to recollect what he had known as a boy. The task was often a hard one, but his desire to benefit his charge induced him to persevere, when probably he might otherwise have abandoned the attempt.

Month after month passed away, and Dick and Charley continued to live their Robinson Crusoe style of life without interruption, and in happy ignorance of all that was going on in the world.

CHAPTER FIVE

AT DEATH'S DOOR

"How many years have we been here, Dick?" asked Charley. "It seems to me a great many, for I was a very little fellow when you first took charge of me, and now I am a strong big chap."

"Bring me the bundle of sticks and I will tell you," said Dick; "for I have not thought of reckoning lately, though I have kept the score as carefully as at first." Charley went and brought several sticks tied together and notched all over. Dick examined them.

"It's three years to-day, according to my reckoning, since we were put on shore. To my mind we ought to thank God, who has taken such care of us all this time. I should not mind, however, getting away soon, for your sake. It's time you should be having some book-learning. I don't want you to grow into a poor ignorant fellow like me."

"You are not ignorant, Dick," said Charley. "You taught me all I know, and I have no greater fancy for books than you have."

"But, Charley, I have another reason for wishing to get

away," said Dick. "You see our clothes are pretty nearly worn out, and I have only stuff enough to make one more suit for you and one for myself, and you will grow out of yours pretty fast, as you have done the others. Then we may not always find provisions as plentiful as we have generally up to this time; birds don't come to the island as they did once, and I fancy that even the fish don't bite as freely along shore as they used to do. I have been thinking of building a larger boat, so that we may go farther off. That wreck which drove on the reef six months ago has given us plenty of stuff for timbers and planking, as well as canvas for sails, and now you are big enough to help me, I shall get on faster than when I built the small one."

Charley replied that he should be glad to do whatever Dick wished, and would try to learn carpentering. Dick accordingly set to work to build a large boat. The undertaking was, however, more difficult than he had expected, and at last he had to abandon his design, and, instead, to try and enlarge the little punt, or the coracle rather, which he had constructed some time before.

The two carpenters laboured away every day, when not engaged in shooting or fishing, or otherwise providing for their support.

Dick had husbanded his ammunition, but even that was coming to an end, and though eggs were still to be found, he could not hope longer to shoot many birds, which had become wilder in consequence of hearing the report of his gun.

Among the treasures sent on shore by the pirates was a small keg of tobacco. Dick had used it pretty freely for the first year or two, but latterly, finding that it must also come to an end, he put himself on an allowance, and only smoked a pipe

W. H. G. Kingston

occasionally when his day's work was over, and he took his seat with Charley on the bench under the porch in front of their hut. Charley had asked one day why he should not smoke too.

"A very good thing for grown men like me," answered Dick, "but very bad for little boys. When you have been at sea a dozen years or so, you may try if you like it. If it was to do you good I would share my last plug with you—you know that, Charley."

"Yes, indeed I do," was the answer, and Charley never again asked for tobacco.

They were seated, as I was saying, within the porch one evening, when Dick, whose eyes were turned towards the boat, drawn up on the beach in the little bay in front of them, observed—

"I have a fancy for taking a cruise farther out than we have been yet; we shall get bigger fish, and not lose so many lines and hooks. I am afraid we shall soon have nothing else but fish to live upon, and though they are not bad food, yet, if there was to come a spell of foul weather, such as we have had now and then, we should not be able to get even them. Now what I want is to catch a good quantity, that we may salt them down for a store, should there be nothing else to be got."

Charley was well pleased with the thoughts of a longer cruise, and early in the morning, having carried down some cocoa-nuts and boiled roots, with a few eggs and fish, which they cooked over night, they launched their curiously-built boat. She was, as Dick observed, a good one to run before a breeze, but where it came to sailing with the wind abeam, she was apt to go as fast to leeward as she did ahead. He, however, had made three oars, two of which he pulled himself, while he had taught Charley to steer with the third.

Though the wind blew off the land, it being light, Dick had no doubt he should easily be able to pull back again. Having examined the reefs from a height in the neighbourhood, and easily making his way among them, he reached the outer circle. Here he let down a big stone, to serve as an anchor, attached to a long rope; but he found the water deeper than he had expected, though, as the stone touched the bottom, he hoped that it would hold the boat.

The lines had not been long over the side before Charley hooked a big fish, larger than he had ever before seen. Dick helped him to haul it in, though, as he was so doing, it nearly broke away. Dick caught two or three, then Charley got another bite; he was again obliged to cry out for Dick's assistance. Dick saw that, from the size of the fish, skill would be required to capture it, and he continued playing it a considerable time, before he ventured to haul it up to the boat. On getting it on board he found that the hook was twisted, and some more time was employed in putting on a new one. Thus eager in and occupied with the sport, Dick did not observe that the boat was slowly drifting along the reef, away from the entrance, by which alone he could regain the shore. The wind was also increasing, though as the sea was smooth he did not discover this. At length, looking up, he observed the position of the boat, and on going to the bows, found that the cable was slack and the stone no longer at the end of it. It had been cut through. Quickly hauling in the cable and the fish-lines, and telling Charley to take the oar to steer, he began pulling hard to regain the passage through the reefs. A strong current was, however, against him, as was the wind, which had shifted slightly, and though he exerted himself to the utmost, he could make no way.

"I have been so long ashore that I have forgotten my seamanship, and have done a very lubberly thing," he said, as he tugged away. All his efforts were of no avail to urge the heavy tub-like boat against the forces opposed to her. She drifted farther and farther away from the land, and the farther she got the more she felt the influence of the breeze; while the sea also, though smooth near the land, began to tumble and toss in a way which made Dick feel more uncomfortable than he had ever before been in his life. The wind at the time blew only a moderate gale, but he could not help acknowledging that the craft he had been so proud of was very ill able to contend with the heavy sea which was rapidly getting up.

"There's no help for it, and I don't want the craft to capsize. I must run before the breeze, and may be it will shift, and we shall be able to get back again—but if not! well, I won't think of that," said Dick, to himself. "I must keep my own spirits up, for Charley's sake. It will be hard, however, for the poor little chap to lose his life after being saved from the sinking ship and those villainous pirates. For myself I don't care; I have well known ever since I came to sea that any day what happens to so many might happen to me."

The heavy boat, though flat-bottomed, behaved better than might have been expected. Dick, who had taken the helm, steered carefully, keeping right before the seas. As he had not communicated his fears to Charley, the boy was delighted with the way in which she flew over the foaming waters.

"I didn't think you were going to give me such a sail as this, Dick," he exclaimed.

"No more did I, Charley," answered Dick. "Maybe we shall not get back as soon as we wish, but the weather looks fine. I hope we may, some day or other."

Dick, however, was disappointed. The wind continued to freshen, and he was compelled to stand on, fearing the risk of making another attempt to regain the shore.

Night came on. He told Charley to take some food; but he was too much occupied himself to eat. He then, making the boy lie down near him, covered him up with a piece of canvas.

All night long he sat steering his boat and praying that the wind might not further increase. As day dawned he cast a hurried glance astern; the land was not to be seen. He had no compass, and even should the wind change, he would have difficulty in regaining so small a spot. He had not the heart to awake Charley, fearing that he would be frightened on finding himself out of sight of land. At length, however, the boy got up and gazed about him with an astonished look.

"Why, Dick, what has become of our island?" he exclaimed. "You never told me you were going to leave it!"

"I wish I had never done so," said Dick. Charley saw that his friend looked anxious.

"I don't know if we are in any danger; but if we are, remember, Dick, that God took care of us on the raft, and can just as well take care of us now. That's what you have taught me; and so I will pray to Him, and I am sure He will hear me."

"Do, Charley, do," said Dick; "and I'll mind the ship."

All that day the boat ran on. Charley insisted on bringing Dick some food, and putting it into his mouth, for he could not venture to leave the helm for an instant. Charley himself seemed perfectly happy, for after getting accustomed to the movements of the boat, the confidence he had in his friend prevented him from thinking of danger.

At length the wind began to fall, and the sea went down, and in a few hours a perfect calm came on. The boat floated without movement.

Dick determined, after he had had a few hours' sleep, to try and pull back. He slept longer than he expected, and Charley, who sat watching by his side, would not awake him. When at last he did open his eyes, it was nearly dark. A thin mist spreading over the ocean and obscuring the stars, he had no means of ascertaining in what direction to pull.

"I might be working away all night, and find that I had only gone farther from the island," he observed. "You and I, Charley, will keep watch and watch. You shall take one hour and I three; that will be about the proper proportion, seeing that I am about three times as old as you are, and want less sleep." So the night passed by.

At last the sun rose, his beams dispersed the mist, and Dick, seizing the oars, began to pull away lustily in the direction he supposed the island to be. Suddenly a crack was heard—one of his oars had gone—he took the steering oar, but that in a few minutes went also.

"It cannot be helped, Charley," he said. "We must trust to Him who knows well how to take care of us."

The boat lay motionless. Hour after hour and day after day passed away. Dick, as he had before done, gave Charley the largest portion of provisions and water, he himself taking barely enough to support life. He felt, too, very sorrowful, thinking of the fate which he feared might be in store for the poor little boy, on whom he had bestowed all the love of his big and tender heart.

As long as he had strength he stood up and gazed around, in the hopes of seeing a sail approaching. At length he sat down, and felt that he should not be able to rise any more. Charley brought him some water.

"Drink it, Dick," he said; "it will do you good; I am not thirsty."

Dick took a few drops; they revived him, and once more he rose to his feet, holding on by the mast. As he turned his eye to the northward it fell on a sail; he gave a shout of joy, though his voice sounded hollow in his own ears. "Charley," he said, "she is coming this way; pray to God she may not change her course."

So eager was he that he forgot his weakness, and continued standing up, watching the vessel, which came on, bringing up the breeze. He was now sure she would pass near where the boat lay. On and on she came.

"She is an English ship, by the cut of her sails!" he exclaimed. "Charley, my boy, we are saved. I don't think I could have held out many hours longer, and you would not have been far after me."

The stranger approached. It was evident, from the way she was steering, that they were seen; still Dick could not help shouting out as loud as his weak voice would allow. The stranger hove-to, and a boat was lowered.

"I hope they are not pirates," said Charley, "like the others."

"I hope not; but if they are we shall soon find out, and we

can but ask them to put us ashore again; for depend on it they will know the whereabouts of our island."

This was said while the boat was approaching.

"What strange craft is that?" said the officer in command of the boat, examining Dick's wonderful specimen of naval architecture.

Dick explained that he and the boy had been out fishing, and been blown off the island, of which they had been the sole occupants for some years.

"We will hear more about it when we get you on board," said the officer, a fine-looking young man, in a kind voice, observing Dick's exhausted condition.

With the assistance of the crew Dick was lifted into the boat, for he had scarcely strength remaining to move, though Charley scrambled on board by himself. Dick heard from one of the crew, as the boat pulled towards the ship, that she was the *Dolphin*, Captain Podgers, bound round Cape Horn.

"We've two petticoats aboard—the skipper's wife and daughter, so your youngster won't want for nurses to look after him," said the man who told Dick this. "To my mind, however, he'll be best off with the young lady, for t'other's a curious one, and it will depend what humour she's in how she will treat him."

The officer helped Charley up the side, and Dick was hoisted on deck after him. When placed on his feet he sank down, unable to stand.

"He is almost starved," said the doctor, who now appeared. "Take him below, and I will attend to him. But the youngster seems in good case."

"Glad you say so, sir," murmured Dick. "I could not let him want while there was food to be had, and I hope they'll be kind to him aboard, for his parents are gentlefolks, and he wasn't brought up to the hard life he's had to lead of late." Dick said this that Charley might be treated with more consideration than might otherwise have been the case. He was not disappointed; indeed, though roughly clad, the boy had the look and air of a young gentleman.

The captain, a stout, burly man, and his wife, Mrs Podgers, a much stouter woman, already mentioned, now appeared from below, followed by a slight, fair, delicate-looking girl, who offered a strong contrast to her parents—if such could possibly be the relationship they bore to her.

"Let me look at the little fellow," said Mrs Podgers, as she waddled to the gangway, where Charley was still standing near the third mate. "He don't seem as if he had been starved; yet I was told that he and the man were a whole week in the boat without anything to eat. But bring him into the cabin, Mr Falconer; I want to hear all about it." Mrs Podgers, as she spoke, gave Charley a kiss, for which he seemed in no way grateful. He showed less objection, however, to the same treatment from the young lady, and willingly followed her into the cabin, keeping close to her, and at a distance from the stout captain and his wife. Finding, however, that Mrs Podgers did not again attempt to kiss him, he became more reconciled to her, and did good justice, while sitting next to Miss Kitty, to the ample supper placed before him.

Mrs Podgers, and more especially the young lady, listened with great interest to his account of his adventures, and he apparently made his way into the good graces of the elder personage. "Well, Kitty," she said, "as he is too young to go and live among the men forward, and seems well-behaved, if you like to look after him, he may remain in the cabin, and you can teach him to read; which if he's the son of gentlefolks he ought to know how to do, and it will be an amusement to you, my dear." Miss Kitty said she should be very happy to take care of the boy, and asked him if he wished to remain.

"Yes, with you," he answered, looking up in her face, "but you'll let me go and see Dick whenever he wants me?"

"Oh, yes, as often as you like," she answered; "and I am glad to find that you are grateful to one who seems to have devoted himself to you; for if we are not grateful to our earthly friends, we are still less likely to be grateful to our heavenly Friend."

"I know whom you mean," said Charley, nodding to her. "Dick has told me about Him; He took care of us all the time we were on the island and in the boat, and Dick has taught me to pray to Him every night and morning, and I shouldn't be happy if I didn't."

"I am very, very glad to hear of that," observed Miss Kitty, pressing the boy's hand. "We shall be friends, Charley."

Honest Dick, who had meantime been placed in a hammock, hearing that Charley was in good hands, felt satisfied about him, though still he begged the doctor to let him have a look at the boy as soon as possible, to assure himself that he was all right.

CHAPTER SIX

CAPTAIN PODGERS

The *Dolphin* under all sail was making rapid progress to the southward.

I have not hitherto mentioned the fact that I was the little Charley I have been speaking of; indeed, so indistinct is my recollection of the earlier events I have described, that had it not been for Dick, I could have known very little about them. Dick soon recovered, and I was delighted when, on having made my way forward, I found myself again with him. He scanned me all over, as if to ascertain whether any harm had come to me during our long separation. I assured him that I was all right, and was loud in my praise of Miss Kitty, though I was less complimentary to Mrs Podgers and the captain.

"They are not nice people," I observed; "drink nasty rum, quarrel and fight, and then kiss and hug; then quarrel and fight again."

My description was a correct one. Mrs Podgers, indeed, had come to sea sorely against her husband's will, simply because she would, and had brought Miss Kitty, who had just come from school, with her—to save the expense of keeping her at home. Miss Kitty was evidently very unhappy, and did not at all like the life she had to lead. She was as refined in appearance, manners, and feelings, as Mrs Podgers was coarse in all three; but the captain, though fat and addicted to rum-drinking in large quantities, and somewhat sulky in his cups, was not nearly as bad as his wife. He was, moreover, greatly tried, both in the cabin by her, and on deck by his unruly crew: the latter was, indeed, about as rough a set of fellows as ever collected on board ship. The first and second mates were not unfitted, by the ready use they made of their fists, to manage them, but the third mate, Edward Falconer, who had brought Dick and me on board, differed from them greatly. He was refined in his appearance and manners, and gentle in his behaviour, though there was, at times, a look in his eye which showed that he was not lacking in spirit and daring.

The *Dolphin*, besides being bound on a whaling cruise, was a "Letter of Marque," by which she had the right, without being considered a pirate, to take and plunder any of the enemy's ships she might fall in with; but when Mrs Podgers, with Miss Kitty, came on board, the crew, suspecting that the captain intended to confine himself to the more pacific of the two occupations, were very indignant, and a mutinous and discontented spirit arose among them.

The captain never from the first took to me.

"I am bothered enough with women, and don't want a brat in the cabin into the bargain," he growled out one day when angry with his wife.

"Oh, but the little boy loves me so much," said Mrs Podgers, drawing me towards her. "Don't you, Charley?"

"No, I can't say I do," I answered; for Dick had charged me

always to speak the truth. "But I love Miss Kitty, that I do, for she is sweet and pretty, and that's what you know you are not;" and I broke away from her and ran up to the young lady.

"Ungrateful little wretch!" exclaimed Mrs Podgers. "Then out of the cabin you shall go, and live with your equals forward."

"Yes, let him go at once," said the captain, "or you will be changing your mind."

"Not likely, after what he has said to me," exclaimed Mrs Podgers. "I would pull his ears, as he deserves, that I would."

Poor Kitty looked very much frightened, and held me close to her. "Oh, don't, Mrs Podgers, pray don't; the little boy did not intend to be naughty, and I will take care of him, and teach him better manners if you will let me."

"No, Miss, I will do no such thing," answered Mrs Podgers, her anger in no way diminished.

"Take him on deck at once, and tell the man who came with him to look after him. If he goes overboard that's his own fault, not mine. I would have been a mother to him, but I cannot stand ingratitude, and he has no claim on my sympathy and affections, as you have, Kitty my dear."

Poor Kitty gave no responsive glance to this remark, but turned away her head, and taking me by the hand led me to the companion stair, whence we went up on deck.

Mr Falconer, who was officer of the watch, stepped up as she appeared. She told him with tears in her eyes what had occurred.

"It is what might be expected," he observed; "but let me entreat you not to be anxious about the little boy. You shall see him as often as you wish, and I suspect that he will be as well off with the honest fellow who had charge of him as he would with those people in the cabin."

I did not understand at the time that there was anything peculiar in his remarks, or that Miss Kitty seemed to place far more confidence in him than she did in captain and Mrs Podgers. I only understood that I was to go back to Dick, and of that I should have been heartily glad, had not my satisfaction been mitigated by the idea that I should be thus separated from Miss Kitty, whose amiability and gentleness had greatly attracted me.

"Well, Charley, we will look after you," said Dick, when I went forward. "There's a vacant berth next to mine, and I'll put your bedding in it. But I am afraid, boy, your manners won't be improved by your new shipmates."

Dick was right, for while I was rapidly increasing my vocabulary of English words, I learned to use some of the expressions constantly issuing from the sailors' mouths, without knowing their meaning, or having any idea of their vileness.

At length, one day, when seated in the forecastle with Dick, I uttered several in succession, highly pleased with my own proficiency. Dick looked at me hard.

"Charley, do you know those are very bad words you are saying?" he exclaimed; "I didn't think you knew such."

"Why, Dick, I heard you say them yourself the other day," and I reminded him of several occasions on which he had uttered some of the words I had made use of.

"Did I, Charley? are you sure of it?" he asked, evidently considering whether I had brought a true or false accusation against him.

"Certain sure, Dick," I said.

"Well, now, I am very sorry for that, and mind, Charley, though you hear other people say what is bad, or see them do what is bad, it is no reason that you should say or do the same; and for my part, Charley, I must clap a preventer-brace on my tongue, and bowse it taut, or those sort of words will, I know, be slipping out. I mind that my good mother used to tell me that I must never take God's name in vain, and that's what I am afraid I have been doing, over and over again. Remember, Charley, if I ever hear you, I'll punish you, and I'll try and break the men of it; it's a shame that they should set such a bad example to a little chap like you, though I am afraid it will be a hard job to stop them."

Dick was as good as his word. From that day forward I never heard him utter an oath, though several times a round one rose to his lips. I at first was not so careful, but the rope's-ending he gave me made me recollect for the future. The men cried shame when they saw him beating me, and were not a little astonished when he told them that it was their fault, and that of course if they swore the little chap would swear also. After this, I really believe that several of them, rough as they were, restrained themselves when I was within hearing, though the greater number went on as before.

Both on and after crossing the line the *Dolphin* was frequently becalmed for several days at a time, which did not improve the captain's temper, nor that of the crew either. The voyage therefore was greatly prolonged. I was more with Miss Kitty than I had expected, for the captain and his wife very frequently, after indulging in potations long and deep, fell asleep in the cabin. On such occasions she used to make her escape on deck. She never seemed tired of watching the flying-fish skimming over the ocean, or the dolphins swimming by, or the sea-birds which passed in rapid flight overhead, or watching the magnificent frigate-bird as it soared on high, and then shot down into the ocean to grasp its finny prey.

Sometimes, however, I used to wonder what she could be looking at when Edward Falconer was by her side gazing with her over the ocean. To be sure, there were the stars glittering above, or the moon with her path of silvery light cast across the vast expanse of water, and she and he seemed never tired of gazing at it. Sometimes on such occasions she held me by her hand, and seemed always to wish to have me near her. I at first was not able to understand what she and the young mate were talking about, but in time, as I learned more English, I perhaps comprehended more than they supposed.

"I have been a wild, wayward, careless fellow, Kate," I heard Mr Falconer say one evening as he stood by Miss Kitty's side. "Instead of remaining at college, and taking advantage of the opportunities I possessed of rising in the world, I spent all my means, and then, to the grief of an excellent father, shipped on board a merchantman as a sailor before the mast. My knowledge of mathematics soon enabled me to become a better navigator than the captain himself, while I rapidly acquired a knowledge of seamanship, as from having been accustomed all my life to boating and yachting, I was at once perfectly at home. I soon became a mate, but I spent all my pay, and was glad to ship on board the *Dolphin*, the first vessel I could find which had a vacant berth. Had I known the character of the master and the officers with whom it was to be my lot to associate, I should certainly, as you may suppose, have avoided her. I had already found, like the prodigal son, that I had dry husks alone to eat, and bitterly mourning my folly, had, even before the ship sailed, contemplated returning home on the first opportunity and seeking my father's forgiveness, when you came on board and I began to breathe a new existence."

"You need not tell me more, Edward," said Kitty. "I cannot bear the thoughts of having prevented you from doing what you considered right, and right it was, I am sure. You must not think of me; oh, let me urge you to go home, and occupy the position which from your education and family you should properly enjoy, for surely your father will receive you thankfully, and forgive your offences. As for me—humanly speaking—I am helpless; but I am not without hope—for I know in whom I trust. Were I not confident that God watches over and takes care of all who have faith in that love which induced Him to give us the greatest gift He could bestow on perishing sinners, I should indeed be miserable."

Much more was said which I did not hear. Mr Falconer and Kitty took several turns on deck together, and I ran about near them.

Their conversation was interrupted by the sudden appearance of Mrs Podgers' head at the companion-hatch, as in an angry tone she summoned the young lady below. The mate walked aft, and I scampered forward to rejoin Dick.

CHAPTER SEVEN

THE FIRE

The *Dolphin* being greatly in want of water, put into the Falkland Islands to obtain it, as well as beef, which the captain understood could be obtained for the trouble of catching the animals on whose backs it existed.

The shore of the harbour in which we lay was rocky, but beyond it was a wide expanse of partly level, and partly undulating ground, reaching far away in the distance.

Dick told me he would take me on shore to see some of the fun, he being one of the men appointed to shoot the cattle.

Mounted Spaniards, or Indians, with their bolas and lassoes, would have killed them with perfect ease; but, armed as we were, with only heavy muskets which did not always go off, the chances were very great against the desired beef being obtained. Just as we had shoved off, the captain, seeing me in the boat, ordered me back. The men, however, having already begun to give way, pretended not to hear him, and we were soon beyond hailing distance of the ship. In a short time we saw another boat following us. After we had landed, who should step out of her but Miss Kitty and Mr Falconer; he had a gun on his shoulder, but had not intended coming till he found that she wanted to have a walk on shore. Whether or not she had asked leave of Mrs Podgers, I do not know; she did not always consider that necessary when she had a fancy for doing anything.

We pushed on some way inland, and though the herbage was high, it was not thick except in places where there were large tufts of tall tussock-grass, like waving plumes growing out of the earth, while the ground itself was tolerably smooth. We went on till we reached a rocky knoll rising like an island amidst the sea of waving grass that surrounded it. We climbed to the top, that we might discover where the cattle were to be found in greatest numbers. As yet, a few only had been seen, which scampered off before a shot at them could be obtained. Three or four herds were discovered in the distance. The mate, with half the men, agreed to go in one direction and to stalk them down, while Dick and the rest went in another. Miss Kitty said she was tired, and that she would remain on the top of the rock with me till their return. The mate begged to leave with her a flask of water and some biscuits, which he had brought, I suspect, on her account. Not knowing what sort of scenery she might meet with, she had brought her sketch-book, for she was a well-educated girl, and understood music, and a number of other things besides. She laughingly observed that a few strokes would quickly picture the surrounding scenery. She amused herself with copying a huge tuft of the tussock-grass which grew near, and then made me stand and sit, now in one position, now in another, while she took my portrait. Then telling me to play about near her, and to take care not to tumble off the rock, she sat down to meditate. What her thoughts were about I cannot say, but she certainly very often looked in the direction Edward Falconer had gone.

Several shots were heard from time to time. They grew fainter and fainter, as if the cattle had headed off away from the harbour.

The day wore on. The sun was already sinking in the sky.

"I wonder when they will come back?" she said once or twice. "Can you see any one, Charley?"

I looked, but could not distinguish any objects amid the expanse of grass.

A dull booming sound of a ship's gun came from the direction of the harbour, then another and another.

"That is, I suspect, to recall the boats," said Kitty to me. "I could find my way there with you, Charley; but I don't like to leave this spot, lest those who have gone after the cattle on returning might wonder what has become of us."

We waited some time longer—the sun set—the shades of evening drew on. Kitty became very anxious. It was too late now to attempt alone to get back to the boats; and it was evident that we should have to spend the night on the knoll. As there was plenty of tall grass around, I proposed that we should build a hut for ourselves, but, as we had no means of cutting it, we could not carry out my project. Miss Kitty was, as before, casting an anxious gaze around, expecting each moment that some one would appear, when suddenly she exclaimed—

"See, see, Charley! What is that?"

I looked in the direction she pointed, when I saw a dark line of smoke rising out of the plain, curling in wreaths as it ascended towards the sky. It might have been mistaken for mist, had there not appeared below it a thin red line with sharp little forks darting upwards.

"The grass is on fire! Oh, what will become of them?" she exclaimed, seizing my hand, and gazing, with dread and horror in her countenance, at the advancing line of flame and smoke. I did not suppose that we ourselves were in danger; but on looking round I observed the numerous tufts of grass which grew on every side among the rocks.

One part of the mound was composed entirely of bare rock. I pointed it out to my companion. Though we should be almost suffocated with smoke, we might there escape the flames. We hastened to it, and kneeling down, she prayed for protection for me, and for herself, and for Edward—I heard her mention the mate's name—and for the rest.

I was not particularly frightened, because I did not see anything very terrible; only the red line of fire jumping and leaping playfully, and the wreaths of smoke, which looked very graceful as they curled round and round, till at length they formed a dark canopy which spread over the sky.

"They may have been on the other side of the fire," I heard Kitty say; "but then he would have thought of me, and, I fear, have attempted to rush through the flames to my rescue, and Dick will not have forgotten you, Charley. We must pray for them, my boy—we must pray for them."

On came the wave of flame; the whole island from one end to the other seemed on fire. Our communication with the harbour was well-nigh cut off. Though the men in charge of the boats might have seen it approaching, they could not have come to our assistance.

Happily, Kitty's dress was of a thick material, and so was mine, for the weather had been for some time cold, and Dick had made me a winter suit. Kitty saw clearly that the flames would surround the rock, and creep up its sides; and the open space on which we had taken refuge was fearfully small. I fancied that I could hear the roaring and hissing of the flames, they were already so near, when a shout reached our ears.

"They are coming! they are coming!" cried Kitty; "but oh, I fear the fire will overtake them before they can gain the rock. I see them! I see them! It is dreadfully close!" She gasped for breath. Then she rose to her feet, and waved her white handkerchief, hoping that it might be distinguished through the gloom, for she in vain tried to cry out in answer to the shout we had heard. The glare of the approaching fire fell on her figure. At that moment a man dashed up the rock—it was Edward Falconer. He could only utter, "You are safe, dearest!" and sank on the ground. Kitty stooped down and tried to raise him, pouring some water from the flask into his mouth. He speedily revived. Three other men followed him—the first was Dick; he seized me in his arms, and gave me a hug and put me down on the rock, and then he and the rest dashed back towards the flames, and began with their guns to beat and trample down the surrounding grass. The mate joined them, but the flames quickly reached the spot, and in a few minutes we were surrounded by a sea of fire. Dick sheltered me in his arms, and Edward Falconer supported Kitty in the very centre of the rock, turning their backs to the scorching flames from which they attempted to shield us. The smoke curled round our heads, and we had great difficulty in breathing. I could not help crying out from the pain of suffocation, which made Dick almost distracted. He first lifted me up above his head, that I might get more air; and when he could support me no longer, he threw a handkerchief over my face, and held me in his arms as a mother would her child.

How long we stood thus I do not know; it seemed a very long time. At length the fire had burned up all the grass around us, and the smoke grew less. Still it was impossible to reach the harbour, and might be so for many hours to come.

The whole party sat down on the rock, Miss Kitty inviting me to come to her, while Edward Falconer sat by her side.

"As you like, Miss," said Dick; "but I would not give him up to any one else."

"I hope the rest got off safe, as they were not far from the shore," observed one of the men. "But I say, Dick, I wonder what has become of the beasts you and Mr Falconer killed?"

"They must be well roasted, at all events," answered Dick. "The sun won't have been long up either before every bone will be picked clean by the galinasos and other birds."

"It's mighty possible, I'm afraid, that two or three of our fellows have been caught. It will be a cruel job if they are, for though a sailor lays it to his account to get drowned now and then, he doesn't expect to be frizzled into the bargain," observed Pat O'Riley.

They went on joking for some time, notwithstanding the fearful scene they had gone through, and although even at that moment some of their shipmates might be lying scorched to death on the plain below them. I, however, was soon asleep, with my head on Kitty's lap, and therefore cannot say what she and Edward Falconer talked about. All I know is, that before I closed my eyes I saw him endeavouring to shield her from the wind, which blew sharply over the knoll.

At daylight we set out, Edward and Dick insisting on carrying Kitty in a chair formed with their hands, while Pat O'Riley carried me on his shoulders.

W. H. G. Kingston

"Well, Miss Kitty, we had given you up for lost," exclaimed Mrs Podgers, who met us at the gangway.

It struck me, young as I was, that her address did not show much maternal affection.

"Had not Mr Falconer and some of the crew come to our rescue, the boy and I would have been probably burnt to death, but they bravely risked their lives to save ours," answered Kitty, firmly.

A boat was sent back to look for the remainder of the men; some at length arrived, but three could not be found, though search was made for them in every direction. Some thought that they had run away, others that they had been destroyed by the flames. A portion of one ox only was brought on board, but the captain would not wait to obtain more, and having filled up the water-casks, the *Dolphin* again sailed to go round Cape Horn.

We had got very nearly up to the southern end of America, when we met a gale blowing directly against us, which sent us back far away to the eastward and southward. The wind, however, again coming fair, we ran before it under all sail to make up for lost time.

Finding Dick's berth empty one evening after it was dark, and not feeling inclined to sleep, I crept up on deck to be with him, as I had been accustomed to do in more genial latitudes. I found him on the look-out on the forecastle.

"What do you want to see?" I asked, observing that he was peering into the darkness ahead.

"Anything that happens to be in our way, Charley," he answered. "An island, ship, or an iceberg; it would not be pleasant to run our jib-boom against either of the three."

"What is that, then?" I asked, my sharp eyes observing what I took to be a high white wall rising out of the sea.

"Down with the helm!" shouted Dick at the top of his voice. "An iceberg ahead!"

"Brace up the yards!" cried the officer of the watch from aft.

The mast-heads seemed almost to touch the lofty sides of a huge white mountain as we glided by it.

"In another half-minute we should have been on the berg, if it hadn't been for you, Charley," said Dick, when we had rounded the mountain, and were leaving it on our quarter. "I'll back your sharp eyes, after this, against all on board."

CHAPTER EIGHT

JONAS WEBB

We were a long time regaining our lost ground. I remember at length finding the ship gliding over huge glass-like billows, which came rolling slowly and majestically, as if moved upwards and onwards by some unseen power, with deep, broad valleys between them, into which the ship sinking, their sides alone bounded the view from her deck ahead and astern. On the right rose however, above them, a high, rocky headland, which the third mate told Miss Kitty, as she stood on the deck gazing at the shore, was Cape Horn.

"I could fancy it some giant demigod, the monarch of these watery realms," she observed. "He looks serene and good-tempered at present; but how fearful must be these mighty waves when he is enraged, and fierce storms blow across them."

"You are indeed right, Miss Kitty," he answered; "and for my part, on such occasions, I prefer giving his majesty a wide berth and keeping out of sight of his frown. Provided the ship is sound, and the rigging well set up, we have little dread of these vast waves. A short chopping sea is far more dangerous. However, we shall soon be round the 'Cape,' and then I hope for your sake we shall have fine weather and smooth water."

She stood for some time holding on to a stanchion, gazing at the scene so strange to her eyes.

The captain coming on deck to satisfy himself that all was going on properly, the mate stepped forward to attend to some duty. As the former's rubicund visage disappeared beneath the companion-hatch, Mr Falconer returned aft.

"I have been thinking, Edward, that I was wrong to give the reins to my fancy, as I did just now," said Kitty, in her sweet, artless way. "I should have remembered that He who made the world governs the wide ocean—the tides and currents move at His command, and He it is who bids the waters be at rest, or sends the whirlwind sweeping over them. I feel that it is wrong, even in poetry, to assign to beings of the imagination the power which alone belongs to Him. Do you understand me?"

"Yes, though I should not have thought you wrong," answered the young officer, gazing at her with admiration. "But I do understand you, and I am sure that you are right. God is a jealous God, and cannot of course admit of any detraction from His authority by the creatures He has formed. I see that every form of idolatry, whether the idol be worshipped or not, must be offensive to Him—whether men assign His power to others, or attempt to approach Him in prayer through the mediation of saints or angels, when He has told them to draw near to the throne of grace according to the one way He has appointed."

It may seem strange that I should have recollected this conversation. In truth, I did not, and it was not till many years afterwards that I was told of it. Indeed, I may confess once for all, that had I not possessed the advantage of communicating with some of the principal actors, I should have been unable to describe many of the events which occurred at that period of my existence. I remember, however, the captain, and his amiable consort, Mrs Podgers, and the snappish cruel way she spoke to sweet Miss Kitty and Edward Falconer. She appeared, indeed, to detest him, and took every opportunity of showing her dislike by all sorts of petty annoyances. He bore them all with wonderful equanimity, perhaps for Kitty's sake, perhaps because he despised their author. Sometimes, when he came on deck after dining in the cabin, he would burst into a fit of laughter, as if enjoying a good joke, and would continue to smile when Kitty appeared with a look of vexation and pain on her countenance, supposing he must have been annoyed beyond endurance.

We had just doubled the Cape, when another sail was seen crossing our course, now rising up against the clear sky, now sinking so low that only her upper canvas was visible. We approached each other, when the stranger made a signal that she would send a boat aboard us. We also hove-to, and began gracefully bowing away at each other, as if the ships were exchanging compliments. A seaman with his bag stepped on board when the boat came alongside, and offered to remain, if the captain would receive him as a volunteer. The mate who came in the boat, saying he was an experienced hand, and had been in the Pacific several years, the captain at once accepted his services. We gave the mate the last news from England and several newspapers, and he, in return, offered to take any letters our people might have ready to send home. In a short time we each filled, and stood on our respective courses.

From what the mate had said, our captain was eager to have a talk with the new-comer, Jonas Webb by name. The latter said he had gone out many years before in a South Sea whaler, and when on her homeward voyage he had exchanged into the ship he had just left, then outward-bound. Both ships had been very successful in fishing and making prizes, and he had saved a great deal of money. Not content with what he had got, he wished to make more. He had been all along the coast, and knew every port. Among other pieces of information, he told the captain that two South Sea whalers, captured by the Spaniards, lay in the Bay of Conception, and advised that they should be cut out, declaring that it might easily be done, as the harbour was unguarded by forts. I don't think Captain Podgers was fond of fighting, but he was of money, and he believed that by getting hold of these two ships, he should make more than by catching a score of whales.

After this, both fore and aft, the only talk was about the proposed undertaking. Miss Kitty looked very grave, but though she knew the captain would take very good care to remain safe on board, she guessed that Edward Falconer would be sent on the expedition; and, though he made light of it, he had observed that Jonas Webb was wrong with regard to the place being unfortified. Captain Podgers had got angry, and declared that the man, an experienced old sailor, who had just come from thence, must know more than a young fellow, as he was, could do. Mrs Podgers, with a sneer, also remarked that perhaps he would rather not have any fighting, lest he might get a cut across his face, and spoil his beauty, or the smell of gunpowder would make him faint.

I am sure that the third mate was as brave as steel, and did not think a bit about his good looks; but the sting, somehow or other, struck deeper than most of her venomed darts.

Hoisting American colours, we stood in towards an island off the Bay of Conception. Here heaving to, as night closed in, four of the boats were manned under charge of the three mates and the boatswain. Jonas Webb and Dick went in Mr Falconer's boat.

Those who remained on board anxiously watched for their return, expecting, as the night was light, to see them towing out their prizes.

Some hours passed by, when the rattle of musketry and the boom of great guns came over the calm waters.

"Why, that fellow Webb mast have deceived me!" exclaimed the captain, stamping about the deck in a state of agitation. "Falconer was right. There will be more glory, as he will call it, than profit in the expedition. Bah! I cannot afford to lose men."

Eager eyes were looking out for the expected ships. They did not appear, but at last first one boat and then another was seen emerging from the gloom.

"Well, gentlemen, what has become of the whalers?" exclaimed the captain, as the two first mates stepped on deck.

"The Spaniards peppered us too hotly to enable us to tow them out, sir, and the wind afforded no help," was the answer. "I am afraid Mr Falconer's boat, too, has got into a mess—he had taken one of the whalers, but would not leave his prize, though I suspect several of his men were killed or wounded."

"Was Mr Falconer himself hit?" asked Mrs Podgers, who had come up to hear the news.

"I cannot say, ma'am," answered the first mate. "His boat must have been terribly mauled, and I am afraid that she must have been sunk, or that her crew must have been taken prisoners. I cannot otherwise account for his not following us."

I had hold of Miss Kitty's hand. I felt it tremble; she seemed to be gasping for breath.

"You should have gone back and looked for them," said the captain, who had judgment enough to know that the third mate was one of the best officers in the ship.

"Oh! do, do so!" exclaimed Miss Kitty, scarcely aware of what she was saying. "It was cowardly and cruel to leave them behind."

"Not far wrong," growled the captain, who, if not brave himself, wished his subordinates to fight well—as has been the case with other leaders in higher positions.

The mates were returning to their boats when the shout was raised that the fourth boat was appearing. She came on slowly, as if with a crippled crew. Kitty leaned against the bulwarks for support.

"Send down slings; we have some wounded men here," said a voice which I recognised as Dick's.

"Let the others go first," said another voice. "They are more hurt than I am."

Miss Kitty sprang to the gangway and looked over. Three men were hoisted on board; one especially was terribly injured—it was Jonas Webb. The last who appeared was Mr Falconer.

"I am only wounded in the shoulder, though I am faint from loss of blood," he said, in a feeble voice. He spoke so that Kitty might hear him. "We should have got the prize with more help."

Kitty ran to his side to assist him along the deck, not caring what Mrs Podgers or anybody else might say to her. The exertion, however, was too much for him; and if Dick and another man had not held him up, he would have fallen, for Kitty's slight frame could scarcely have supported him. He was taken to his cabin, and after the doctor had attended to the other men he allowed him to examine his wound.

I have not before mentioned our doctor. The men used to say he was only fit for making bread pills, and they, poor fellows, had better means of forming an opinion of his skill than I had. After his visit, Mr Falconer would not let him dress his wound, though he did manage to get out the bullet. It was dressed, however, and Kitty used to say that I was the doctor. I know that I went every day into the cabin with her and Dick, and that we used to put lotions and plaster on his poor shoulder. Mrs Podgers declared that it was very indelicate in her to do so, but Kitty replied that if women were on board ship, it was their duty to attend to the wounded.

We visited the other men who were hurt, especially poor Jonas Webb; but Kitty confessed that his injuries were beyond her skill—indeed, it seemed wonderful that, mangled as he was, he should continue to live on.

The miscarriage of the expedition was owing also to him. Mr Falconer had gallantly carried the prize, got the Spaniards under hatches, and taken her in tow, when, on passing the batteries, Webb's pistol went off. This drew the attention of the garrison to the boat, and they immediately opened a hot fire. Webb was the first struck, and soon afterwards several of the other men were hit. Mr Falconer, who had remained on deck, on this let himself down into the boat to assist in pulling, and, in spite of the hot fire, would have continued doing so, had not the Spaniards broken loose, and, getting hold of some muskets on board, began firing at the boat. Mr Falconer, on being himself wounded, cut the painter, and the boat escaped without further injury.

Dick was very angry with the other officers, and did not mind expressing his opinion of them. I never saw him so put out. He felt much for poor Webb, and I heard him declare that he was very doubtful about Mr Falconer's recovery. If he died, what would become of poor Miss Kitty?

CHAPTER NINE

A MINISTERING ANGEL

Mr Falconer did not die. Kitty asked him to live for her sake, and I dare say he was glad to do so. Dick and the doctor were out of hearing at the time, so that I don't know whether I ought to repeat it.

She often, as she sat by his side, spoke very seriously to him, and used to read the Bible. One day she asked whether he truly believed it to be God's word, and to contain His commands to man. He said he did with all his heart, and that he had always done so.

"Then," she asked, "how is it that you have not always lived according to its rules?"

"First, because I did not read the book," he answered; "and, secondly, because I liked to follow my own will."

"And preferred darkness to light, because your deeds were evil? That is what the Bible says, Edward, and you believe that it is God's word," said Kitty, in a firm voice. "But can you now truly say, 'I will arise and go to my Father, and will say unto him, Father, I have sinned against heaven and before thee, and am no more worthy to be called thy son?'"

She gazed with her bright blue eyes full upon him as she spoke, so innocent and free from guile.

"Indeed, I truly can," he said.

"Hear these words," she continued, turning rapidly over the leaves of the Bible she held before her. "'God so loved the world that he gave his only-begotten Son, that whosoever believeth on him should not perish, but have everlasting life.'"

"The faith, the belief, must be living, active, not a dead faith, and then how glorious the assurance, if we remember what everlasting life means—a certainty of eternal happiness, which no man can take away, and which makes the pains, and sufferings, and anxieties of this life as nothing. I always think of those promises, Edward, whenever I am in trouble, and you know I very often am, and I remember that God says, 'I will never leave thee nor forsake thee.' That, and that alone, has enabled me to endure the dreadful life I have had to lead on board this ship, until I knew that you loved me. But the being possessed of that knowledge, though it affords me unspeakable happiness, does not, I confess, make me more free from anxiety than I was before. Then I knew that nothing could take away what I possessed, because it was treasured in my own heart; but now I cannot help feeling anxious on your account—exposed to numberless dangers as you are, and must be, in the horrid work such as I understand this ship is to be engaged in. When that dreadful woman insisted on my accompanying her, I understood that the ship was to make an ordinary voyage, visiting interesting lands, trading with the natives, and catching whales. Had I known the truth I would have resisted her authority, and gone out as a governess or into service as a nursery-maid, or done anything rather than have come on board. But left an orphan and penniless, and under her guardianship, so she asserted, I

W. H. G. Kingston

thought it my duty to obey her. I do not regret it now," she added, quickly; "but I felt that you must have been surprised at finding me dependent on such a person as Mrs Podgers. I have never told you my history—I will do so. When, about ten years ago, my dear mother was dying, just as I was six years old, this woman was her nurse, and pretended to be warmly attached to her. My father, Lieutenant Raglan, having married against the wishes of his family, they, considering that my mother, though highly educated and attractive, was inferior to him in birth and fortune, cast him off, and refused to hold any further communication with him. Just before the time I speak of, he sailed for the East India station, and my dear mother being left at a distance from her own friends, who resided in the West Indies, she had no one of her own station, when her fatal illness attacked her, to whom she could confide me. When, therefore, her nurse promised to watch over me with the tenderest care, and to see that I was educated in a way suitable to my father's position in society, and to restore me to him as soon as he returned, she thankfully left me and all the property she possessed under her charge. Such is what her nurse, now Mrs Podgers, has always asserted. Providentially, my mother had written to a lady, Mrs Henley, at whose school she herself had been educated, saying, that it was her express wish that I should be under her charge until I was sixteen, although I was to spend my holidays with nurse till my father's return. I suspect, that at the last, my poor mother had some doubts about leaving so much in the power of a woman of inferior education; and I remember seeing her write a paper, which she got the respectable old landlord of the house and his son to witness, and it was to be sent, on her death, to my kind friend, Mrs Henley. That paper, or one very like it, I afterwards saw my nurse destroy.

"On my mother's death, I was sent to Mrs Henley, my nurse insisting that I should spend the holidays with her. For the first year or two she was very kind, and I had nothing to complain of; but after she married Captain Podgers, her conduct changed very much, I suspect in consequence of her having taken to drinking. I did not find this out at the time, though I thought her occasionally very odd. She insisted that she was my guardian, and showed me my mother's handwriting to prove her authority; and I felt that it was my duty to obey her, though I lived in hopes that by my father's return I should be freed from her control.

"Year after year passed by. Then came the account of the capture and destruction of his ship and loss of many of her officers, though no information as to his fate could be obtained. All I knew, to my grief, was that he did not return. Still I have a hope amounting almost to confidence that he is alive. The thought that I might possibly meet with him made me less unwilling than I should otherwise have been to obey Mrs Podgers' commands to accompany her on the voyage she was about to make. Her sole motive, I suspect, in wishing me to go, was to save the expense of my continuing at school. Still I wonder sometimes how I could have ventured on board, suspecting, as I had already done, the hypocritical character of the woman who had pretended to be so devoted to my mother and me."

"You have, at all events, proved an inestimable blessing to me," said the young officer. "Even when I first saw you, I could not believe that you were really the daughter of such people as the captain and his wife."

I do not know that I had before thought much about the matter, but when I heard now, for the first time, that Miss Kitty was not related to the captain and his wife, I felt a sort of relief, and could not help exclaiming, "Oh, I am so glad!" She smiled as she looked at me, but she made no reply either to mine or Mr Falconer's remark. She gave us both, I have no doubt, credit for sincerity.

Although our visits to the wounded mate occupied a good deal of our time—I say our visits, for I always accompanied Miss Kitty—we did not neglect the other wounded men.

We went, indeed, to see poor Jonas Webb several times a day. Sorely wounded as he was, he yet could listen to what Miss Kitty said to him, though he was too weak and suffering to utter more than a few words in reply. She one day, finding him worse, asked him solemnly if he was prepared to meet his God.

"What! do you think I am dying, young lady?" he groaned out, in a trembling voice.

"The doctor says that he has never known any one wounded as badly as you are to recover," she said, in a gentle, but firm voice.

"Oh, but I cannot die!" he murmured. "I have made well-nigh five hundred pounds, and expected to double it in this cruise, and I cannot leave all that wealth. I want to go home, to live at my ease and enjoy it."

"You cannot take your wealth with you," she answered.

Without saving more, she read from the Bible the account of the rich man and Lazarus. She then went on to the visit of the wealthy young lawyer to Jesus, and paused at the reply of the Lord; she repeated the words, "How hardly shall they that have riches enter into the kingdom of God. For it is easier for a camel to go through a needle's eye than for a rich man to enter into the kingdom of God."

"Now," she continued, "you have been trusting in the wealth which, with so much toil and danger, you have been collecting, to enjoy a life of ease and comfort on shore. Suppose God said to you, 'Thou fool, this night thy soul shall be required of thee!' as He does to many; can you face Him?"

"But I don't see that I have been a bad man. I have always borne a good character, and, except when the blood was up, and I have been fighting with the enemy, or when I have been on shore, may be for a spree, I have never done anything for which God could be angry with me."

"God looks upon everything that we do, unless in accordance with His will, to be sinful. He does not allow of small sins any more than great sins; they are hateful in His sight; and He shows us that we are by nature sinful and deserving of punishment, and that, as we owe Him everything, if we were to spend all our lives in doing only good, we should be but performing our duty, and still we should have no right in ourselves to claim admittance into the pure, and glorious, and happy heaven He has prepared for those alone who love Him. He has so constituted our souls that they must live for ever, and must either be with Him in the place of happiness, or be cast into that of punishment. But, my friend, Jesus loves you and all sinners, and though God is so just that He cannot let sin go unpunished, yet Jesus undertook to be punished instead of you, and He died on the cross and shed His blood that you might go free of punishment. If you will but trust in Him, and believe that He was so punished, and that, consequently, God no longer considers you worthy of punishment, but giving you, as it were, the holiness and righteousness which belong to Christ, will receive you into that holy heaven where none but the righteous can enter."

The wounded man groaned and answered slowly, "I am afraid that I am a sinner, though I have been trying to make out that I am not one. But I really have had a very hard life

W. H. G. Kingston

of it, and no good example set me, and shipmates around me cursing and swearing, and doing all that is bad; and so I hope if I do die, as you say I shall, that God won't keep me out of heaven."

"Jesus Christ says, 'There is only one way by which we can enter; there is but one door.' 'I am the Way, the Truth, and the Light.' 'He that believeth on him is not condemned, but he that believeth not is condemned already, because he hath not believed on the name of the only-begotten Son of God.' Jesus also says, 'He that heareth my word, and believeth on him that sent me, hath everlasting life, and shall not come into condemnation, but is passed from death unto life;' and again, 'Believe on the Lord Jesus Christ, and thou shalt be saved.' Jesus came not to call the righteous, or those who fancy themselves good enough to go to heaven, as you have been doing, but sinners, to repentance—those who know themselves to be sinners. Think how pure and holy God is, and how different you are to Him, and yet you must be that holy as He is holy to enter heaven. Christ, as I have told you, gives you His holiness if you trust to Him; and God says, 'Though your sins be as scarlet, they shall be white as snow; though they be red like crimson, they shall be as wool;' and, 'As far as the east is from the west, so far will I put your sins from me.' Believe what God says; that is the first thing you have to do. Suppose Jesus was to come to you now, and, desperately wounded as you are, tell you to get up and walk; would you believe Him, or say that you could not? He said that to many when He was on earth, and they took Him at His word, and found that He had healed them. There was, among others, a man with a withered hand. When He said, 'Stretch forth thine hand,' the man did not say, 'I cannot,' but stretched it forth immediately. Just in the same way, when God says, 'Believe on the Lord Jesus Christ, and thou shalt be saved,' do believe on Him, and trust to Him to fulfil His promise. God never deceives any one; all His words are fulfilled."

Day by day the young girl spoke to the dying seaman, and, though witnessing scenes abhorrent to her feelings, influenced by God's grace, she overcame her repugnance, and faithfully continued to attend him. She had the satisfaction of hearing him cry, "Lord, be merciful to me a sinner!" and confess that he had a full hope of forgiveness, through the merits of Jesus alone.

Two of the other men, though apparently not so severely injured as Webb, owing to the ignorance of the surgeon, sank from their wounds. They died as they had lived, hardening their hearts against the Saviour's love.

Had Miss Kitty not been very firm, Mrs Podgers would have prevented her from attending the mate or the other wounded men.

Mr Falconer, though for some time confined to his cabin, was at length able to get on deck.

"Glad to see you about again," said the captain, as he appeared, in his usual gruff but not unkind tone. "When I brought the ladies aboard, I didn't think that they'd prove so useful in looking after the sick; though I doubt if she," and he pointed with his thumb over his shoulder at his wife, "has troubled you much with her attentions."

Before the mate could speak, Mrs Podgers waddled up to him. "Well, Mr Falconer, you've found your way out of your cabin at last," she said, in her nasty wheezy tone. "I should have thought that when an officer was only slightly hurt, as you were, he might have managed to return to his duty before this."

The mate said nothing, but the remark made Miss Kitty very angry. I should have said, that as Mrs Podgers would not allow me on the quarterdeck, the appearance of the bows in her bonnet above the companion-hatch was the signal for me to escape among my friends forward; and that it was from Dick, who was at the helm, I afterwards heard of the unpleasant remarks made by that most unattractive of females.

CHAPTER TEN

WHALING AND FIGHTING

The *Dolphin*, after her first ill-success at privateering, stood away from the coast towards a part of the ocean where it was expected that whales would be found. Look-outs were at the mast-head.

I was sitting with Dick forward, for as Mrs Podgers was sunning herself on deck, I was keeping out of her way. Miss Kitty was reading, and Mr Falconer was pacing up and down, as officer of the watch, taking care not to approach her till Mrs Podgers should dive below. Most of the crew were knitting and splicing, spinning yarns, or performing other work, of which there is always plenty to be done on board ship, while some few of them were lying lazily about, doing nothing.

I have not before mentioned a personage who was dubbed the officer of marines, Lieutenant Pyke. His figure was tall and thin, as the captain's was short and broad, and though their noses were much of the same colour, being as red as strong potations and hot suns could possibly make them, Lieutenant Pyke's was enormously long. He was now engaged in drilling twelve of the most ruffianly and ill-conditioned of the crew, whom he called his jollies. They

W. H. G. Kingston

were of various heights and dimensions, and though they wore red coats and belts, knee-breeches and gaiters, and carried muskets, they were, as Dick, who held them in supreme contempt, declared, "as unlike sodgers as they could well be." Lieutenant Pyke, however, was proud of them, and boasted that they would follow him to the cannon's mouth, whenever he led the way.

"Likely enough they will," observed Dick, "because, you see, there's little chance of the lieutenant ever getting there."

He had for some time been drilling these troops of his, as he also occasionally designated the fellows, making them march up and down, and pointing every now and then to an imaginary enemy, whom he ordered them to charge and annihilate, when there came a shout from aloft, "There she blows!" In a moment all the crew jumped to their feet. Our stout captain tumbled up from below, crying out, "Where away!" and four boats being lowered and manned, off they pulled, led by Mr Falconer in the direction in which the look-out pointed. We could see, about a quarter of a mile from the ship, a huge hump projecting three feet out of the water, while from the fore part of the monster's enormous head arose at the end of every ten seconds a white jet of foam.

"There again! there again!" shouted the crew. Away dashed the boats at full speed.

"His spoutings are nearly out," said Dick.

"He is going down," cried others.

Again a spout rose, and we could see the small, as it is called, of his back rise preparatory to his descent.

"His tail will be up directly," said Dick, "and they will lose him, I fear;" but at that moment Mr Falconer's boat dashing on, as he stood up in the boat with his glistening harpoon raised above his head, away it flew with unerring force, and was buried in the side of the huge animal. A loud cheer rose from the men in the boats and those on deck, and the whale, hitherto so quiet, began to strike the water with his vast tail, aiming with desperate blows at his advancing enemies. Now his enormous bottle-nose-shaped head rose in the air—now we saw his flukes lashing the water, his body writhing with the agony of the wound the sharp iron had inflicted. The water around him was soon beaten into a mass of foam, while the noise made by his tail was almost deafening.

Kitty stood eagerly watching the scene, and looking somewhat pale, for it seemed as if the boat could scarcely escape some of those desperate blows dealt around.

I had felt very anxious about my friend.

"Never fear," said Dick; "he knows what he is about. See, it's 'stern all.'"

The boat backed out of the way; the monster's tail rose for an instant and disappeared.

"He has sounded," cried Dick.

Away ran the line. An oar was held up in the boat.

"That means that the line has run out," said Dick.

The nearest boat dashed up, and a fresh line was bent on. That soon came to an end, and another, and yet another was joined to it.

"He has eight hundred fathoms out by this time," shouted

W. H. G. Kingston

Dick, "and if he does not come up soon, he will be lost. But no, it's 'haul in the slack;' he is rising; they are coiling away the line in the tubs."

Directly afterwards the blunt nose of the animal rose from the sea, and a spout was projected high into the air. Mr Falconer's boat was being hauled rapidly towards it. A long lance with which he was armed was quickly buried in the side of the huge creature, going deep down into a vital part. The other boats gathered round it, from each a lance was darted forth, the whale rolling over and over in his agony, and coiling the rope round him, when suddenly, with open jaws, he darted at one of the boats, and then attacked another. Kitty shrieked out with fear, for it was Mr Falconer's boat which was overtaken, and was seen, shattered to fragments, flying into the air, while the other was capsized; and now the whale went so swiftly along the surface, that it seemed he must after all escape. Two of the boats were not yet fastened, and, without stopping to help the men in the water, away they dashed in chase of the whale. Impeded by the shattered boat he was dragging after him, and by several drogues fastened to the lines, he was soon overtaken, when another harpoon and several more lances were darted into his body. Still unconquered, away the animal again went, and up rose his tail: he was attempting to sound, but this his increasing weakness prevented him from doing. Then he stopped, and his vast frame began to writhe and twist about in every possible way, beating the surrounding sea into foam, and dyeing it with his blood. The boats backed out of his way. The captain had sent another boat to the assistance of the men in the water, when it was seen that the one upset was righted, and that the people belonging to the shattered boat had been taken on board her. She soon joined those which were fast to the whale, and when the monster at length lay motionless on the water, assisted them in towing it up to the ship.

Kitty could scarcely conceal her joy when she saw Mr Falconer steering one of the boats. I shouted with satisfaction.

The whale was soon alongside, and the operation of cutting off the blubber, hoisting it on board, and boiling it down in huge caldrons placed on tripods, commenced.

As night came on, the fires lighted under the pots shed a bright glare across the deck on the rigging and on the men at work. I thought them wild and savage-looking enough before, but they now appeared more like beings of the lower world than men of flesh and blood.

"I have no fancy for this sort of work," observed Dick, who was a thorough man-of-war's man. "The decks won't be fit to tread on for another week."

However, we had the decks dirtied in the same way many a time for several weeks after that, being very successful in catching whales.

At last the fighting part of the crew, who were not accustomed to whaling, began to grumble, and wished to return to the coast, to carry on the privateering, or, as Dick called it, the pirating work, which they looked upon as the chief object of the voyage.

Lieutenant Pyke was especially urgent about the matter, and proposed that a descent should be made on some of the towns, which he and his brave troops, he asserted, could capture without difficulty.

On reaching the coast, we brought up in a small bay with a town on its shore.

W. H. G. Kingston

We had not been long at anchor, when in the evening a boat came off, manned by natives, with three Spaniards in her. The captain received them very politely, and introduced them to his wife and Kitty. They seemed highly pleased, and said they had come to trade, taking the *Dolphin* to be a smuggler, many English vessels visiting the coast for the purpose of landing goods free of the high duties imposed on them by the Spanish Government. As many pieces of cloth and cotton as could be found were shown to them as samples. The captain told them that if they would return on board with their dollars, the goods should be ready for them.

Mr Falconer, when he heard of the shameful trick which it was proposed to play the unfortunate Spaniards, was very indignant, and I believe would have warned them if he could. The captain, hearing what he had said, backed by Lieutenant Pyke and one of the other officers, declared that he would shoot him through the head if he did any such thing.

During the night, two boats came off with our former visitors and four others, all bringing a large supply of dollars. On going down below, great was their dismay on finding that they were prisoners, and that, when released, they would have to leave their money behind them and go without the goods.

In the morning, another boat appeared with two more merchants, who were treated in the same way. Altogether, ten thousand dollars were thus stolen from the Spaniards.

"They are breaking the laws of their country," observed Dick to me, "and they deserve punishment. For my part, I don't like this way of doing things; but if Mr Pyke is as good as his word, and was to land with his marines and attack the town, it would be more ship-shape and honourable."

I mention the circumstance to show the abomination of the privateering system, but people generally did not see it in the same light in those days.

A suspicious sail appearing in the offing, the Spaniards were allowed to go on shore, though Lieutenant Pyke declared that if he had his way they should all have been made to pay a heavy ransom first. The anchor was hove up, and we stood out to sea. We were becalmed during the day, while still at a distance from the stranger. As evening approached, a breeze springing up, she neared us, with a black flag flying from her peak. From the cut of her sail and the appearance of her hull, she was an English vessel, fully as large, if not larger, than the *Dolphin*; but there could be no doubt of her character— she was a pirate. The drum beat to quarters, and preparations were made to give her a warm reception. Mrs Podgers and Kitty were sent down into the cockpit, where they might be out of harm's way. It was by this time nearly dark, but still the stranger could be seen gliding towards us through the thickening gloom. Dick took me up and carried me to them, in spite of my entreaties to be allowed to see the fun.

"It will be no fun, Charley, if yonder scoundrels do as they intend, and try to take the ship," he remarked. "At all events, there will be some desperate fighting, and a shot may carry your head off, my boy—so below you must go, whether you like it or not."

Kitty took my hand and drew me towards her as soon as I appeared, thankful that I was not to be exposed to danger.

"I should think the little brat might be made useful, sitting on an ammunition tub," exclaimed Mrs Podgers. "Why should he be more petted than the other boys?"

"No, no!" cried Kitty, holding me fast. "He is younger than

W. H. G. Kingston

they are, and it would be cruel to let him run the risk of being hurt."

We waited for some time, no one speaking; for Mrs Podgers was too much frightened, and Kitty too anxious, to do so. At length there came the dull sound of a gun fired from the other vessel, followed by louder, clearer reports of several discharged by the *Dolphin*. The enemy replied with a still greater number, and several broadsides were soon afterwards rapidly exchanged between the combatants. The firing now ceased. We waited almost breathless to hear it begin again.

CHAPTER ELEVEN

ATTACK ON THE SPANISH HIDALGO

As no wounded men had been brought below, we trusted that the *Dolphin* was having the best of it. At last I begged Kitty to let me go on deck and ascertain how matters were going on.

"No, no, Charley," she answered. "They may again begin firing;" but I saw that she was very anxious herself to learn the state of affairs.

"I will be back again in a minute," I said, and was just escaping from her, when once more the thundering sound of big guns, with the rattle of musketry, broke the silence, and she caught me and held me fast.

The firing went on with redoubled vigour, and cries and shouts reached our ears. The alarm of Mrs Podgers increased.

"O dear, O dear!" she cried out, wringing her hands. "If Podgers was to be hit, what would become of me?"

Once more there was a cessation of the firing.

"Do let me run up, Kitty," I said. "Some of those we care for may be wounded, and the rest too busy to bring them below."

I knew my argument would prevail. "Let him go," said Mrs Podgers. "I do so want to know how the captain is."

I broke from her and climbed up the ladder. I was as active as a monkey, and quickly reached the deck. The fighting lanterns which hung against the bulwarks shed their light across it, and showed me several human forms stretched out motionless. The crew, stripped to their waists, were at the guns, while the officers stood about here and there among them. I caught sight of the captain's stout figure, but I looked in vain for Mr Falconer. I ran forward in hopes of finding him. I had got nearly to the forecastle when the matches were applied to the guns, and as they were discharged a shower of shot came hissing across the deck.

I made my way amidst the shower of shot and bullets and falling blocks, and the horrible din of battle, to the forecastle, where, to my great joy, I saw Mr Falconer directing the foremost guns. Dick at the same moment caught sight of me.

"Charley," he exclaimed, "what business have you here? Go back, boy, and tell the ladies we are all right, and will make the pirate sheer off before long, if we don't take her."

I hurried below with the satisfactory intelligence. Miss Kitty kissed me when I told her I had seen Mr Falconer, and I was somewhat afraid that Mrs Podgers would bestow the same reward upon me when I said that the captain was unhurt.

"I wish he would make haste and sink the ship which has frightened us so much," she observed. "It is a shame that those sort of people should be allowed to live."

Mrs Podgers did not consider that the Spaniards would

probably have said the same of us.

We heard our ship fire several broadsides in rapid succession; then all was silent.

Supposing that the fight was over, I persuaded Miss Kitty again to allow me to run on deck. Reaching it, I caught sight, a short distance off, of the tall masts and sails of the enemy's ship.

At that moment loud cheers burst from the throats of our crew. Gradually the dark sails of our antagonist appeared to be sinking, and wild shrieks and cries came across the waters towards us. Lower and lower the sails sank, and in another minute the spot occupied by the pirate was vacant—she had disappeared beneath the waves. No boat was sent to help the drowning wretches. Mr Falconer proposed going to their assistance.

"No, no!" exclaimed the captain; "they would have robbed us or sent us to the bottom; they don't deserve our pity."

"But they are fellow-creatures, and we should try and save their lives," exclaimed the mate.

"You are too tender-hearted, Falconer; you should not have joined a privateer," was the answer; and the *Dolphin* glided rapidly away from the spot where her foe had gone down.

The surgeon was meantime busy with the wounded men, while five who had been killed were with little ceremony hove overboard. Mrs Podgers and Kitty returned to the cabin. The latter, as before, endeavoured to alleviate the sufferings of the wounded men, and often visited them, attended by Mr Falconer and me, notwithstanding the scoldings she daily got from Mrs Podgers for so doing.

After this, we again stood in for the coast, capturing several Spanish merchant vessels.

Mr Pyke declared that he wanted to find an enemy more worthy of his and his troops' prowess than he had hitherto encountered.

"We will give you a chance," said the captain. "I have discovered from some of the prisoners that there is a town on the shores of a bay not far off, which is unprotected by forts. We may easily make ourselves masters of the place, and shall probably find in it a good store of wealth. But we must be quick about the business, or some troops stationed at no great distance may be down upon us and interfere with our proceedings."

"You may depend upon me for doing my part," answered the lieutenant, drawing himself up.

We made the land early in the day, but hove-to till night, when it was hoped the inhabitants might be taken by surprise. The weather was fine, and the entrance to the harbour broad and safe. We waited till past midnight, and then stood in and came to an anchor. Four boats were ordered to be got ready; Lieutenant Pyke and his marines went in one of them, the others were commanded by the sea officers, with a party of blue-jackets.

I had heard the men talking of what they were going to do, and I thought that I should very much like to see the fun. I knew, however, that neither Dick nor Miss Kitty would approve of my going, and that Mr Falconer was also unlikely to take me, should I ask him to do so. The last boat which left the ship was commanded by the boatswain, a rough but good-natured man, with whom I had become somewhat of a favourite. I watched my opportunity, and slipped in directly after him, and the men, thinking that he intended I should go, allowed me to stow myself away in the bow before he saw me, the darkness favouring my design. The boats shoved off, and away we pulled, with muffled oars, towards the shore.

We landed just outside the town, among wild rocks. No lights were moving about the place, only here and there a few glimmering from the windows. Lieutenant Pyke drew up his marines; the other officers arranged their men in a compact body, I following the rear.

Daylight broke. When all was ready, the first mate ordered us to advance, and, stepping lightly over the ground, we made a rush into the town. There were no gates to stop us and no sentinels on the watch. A sort of town-hall and a church were first entered, and everything they contained, images, silver candlesticks, crucifixes, incense-pans, chalices, and several bags of money, with some silver-mounted guns and pistols, were taken possession of before the inhabitants were awake. We then attacked a large house in which lights were still burning, and where it was supposed the commandant of the place resided. The door yielded to the blows of the marines' muskets, and rushing into a good-sized hall, we saw seated at the end of a long table a thin, tall hidalgo, and on either side of him a fat priest, with two or three other personages. The table was covered with rich plate and numerous flagons and wine-flasks. The party gazed at us with open mouths and staring eyes, but were far too tipsy to utter anything beyond a few expressions of surprise and dismay.

The commandant, rising, tried to draw his sword, but could not find the hilt, and tumbled back into his big armchair; while the fat friars, whose first impulse had been to make their escape, rolled over on the ground, upsetting the hidalgo's chair in their struggles, when all three began

W. H. G. Kingston

kicking and striking out, believing each other to be foes. The rest of the party at once yielded themselves as prisoners. Our men, bursting into loud fits of laughter, let the trio fight on for some time, till our commander, fearing, should we delay longer, that the inhabitants would make their escape, or perhaps assemble and attack us, ordered them to be lifted up and carried off, with their arms bound behind them. It was no easy matter to do this, for the friars were so heavy that it required three stout men to each to set them on their legs.

While a party was left to guard them, the rest proceeded to break into the other houses.

The inhabitants, now aroused from their slumbers by the hubbub, put their heads, with their nightcaps on, out of the windows in all directions, but quickly withdrew them, uttering loud shrieks and exclamations of dismay and surprise. After a little time Dick caught sight of me.

"Charley," he cried out, "what has brought you here?"

"I wanted to see the fun, Dick. I hope you are not angry."

"But I am, though, Charley," he answered; "and though, to my mind, it's dirty work attacking sleeping people, who have never done us any harm, we may have some fighting yet, and you may get knocked on the head. Stick by me, however, and I'll look after you, though you don't deserve it."

I felt ashamed of myself, and took good care to do as Dick told me.

He, with about half the number of our party, now proceeded to one side of the town, while the other marched to the farther end, three or four armed men entering any of the large houses which appeared likely to contain booty worth carrying off. My party had accompanied the marines under Lieutenant Pyke, who was shouting out "he only wished he could see a foe worthy of his steel." As we went along, we came to a small square, at the other side of which a band of some twenty persons appeared, others coming up in the distance. I am not sure that all had arms, though they presented a somewhat military aspect. Our commander ordered the marines to charge them.

"On, lads, on!" cried the lieutenant, waving his sword, but he did not move very fast. The Spaniards, however, seeing the invaders coming, ran off as fast as their legs would carry them, when the lieutenant doubled his speed, waving his sword still more vehemently, and shouting out: "On, brave lads! Death or victory!" By the time he got across the square, no foe was to be seen, and after looking round the corner to ascertain that they had not reassembled, he marched back his men in triumph.

In a short time every house had been ransacked, and, with our booty and prisoners, we returned to the boats and regained the ship, not a shot having been fired nor a life lost.

The commandant having agreed to pay five thousand dollars as his own ransom and that of his companions, one of the fat friars was sent on shore to collect the money, having orders to return by noon. He shook his head, and declared that this was impossible.

"It might take four or five days, perhaps a week, to collect such a sum."

"Very well," said the captain at last. "By sunset, if the ransom is not brought on board, we shall have a fine bonfire out there," and he pointed to the town.

W. H. G. Kingston

"Arra' now, captain, you may as well cook and eat us at once, for sorrow a dollar have ye left us, and all the crucifixes, and candlesticks, and beautiful images, which we might have pledged for the money, stowed away in your hold!" exclaimed the fat friar, betraying his Hibernian origin, and that he had understood every word which had been spoken.

"Are you an Irishman, and living among these foreigners, and pretending to be one of them?" cried the captain. "If I had known that, I would have clapped on another thousand dollars to your ransom."

"Sure, captain, dear, it would have been more charitable to have taken them off," observed the jovial friar. "However, just be after giving me four days, and ye shall resave the dollars all bright and beautiful, though not a quarter of one could all the blessed saints together collect in the whole of our unfortunate town and the circumjacent country."

The friar's eye twinkled as he spoke. At last he proposed paying even a larger sum, provided that the captain would prolong the time to five days for its collection. Captain Podgers, eager to get more money, and not suspecting treachery, agreed to the proposal, and Fra Patricio, chuckling in his sleeve, prepared to take his departure.

"Captain, dear," he said, turning round with a comical look as he reached the gangway, "ye haven't got a bottle of potheen, the raal cratur, have ye? It would just be after comforting me in my trouble."

A bottle of Irish whiskey being handed to the friar, he tucked it away in his sleeve, and his boat pulled off towards the shore.

Mr Falconer, who understood Spanish, shortly after this informed the captain that he had discovered, from the prisoners' conversation, that the object of Friar Patrick in asking for more time to collect the ransom, was that troops might be sent for to protect the town. The captain replied that he would hang his prisoners if any such trick was played.

We remained two days longer, and no news came from the Irish friar.

Our prisoners were well supplied with eatables and drinkables and tobacco, and appeared perfectly happy, talking freely among themselves, as they sat at table and smoked their cigarettes. Mr Falconer, though unwilling to be an eavesdropper, could not help hearing what they said, and as he had prudently not let them discover that he knew Spanish, they did not suspect that he understood what they said. He was sitting writing in his own cabin, which opened on the gun-room, when he heard one of them remark that, in a couple of days, at furthest, the tables would be turned, and that those who were now their masters would be prisoners, or hung up at the yard-arms of their frigate.

"Which, pirates as they are, will be their just fate," observed another. On this, the rest of the party laughed grimly.

"The ladies we cannot hang, though."

"No; they can be sent to a nunnery, or perhaps you, Seignor Commandant, who are a bachelor, would wish to wed the fat widow."

Some remarks were made about Miss Kitty, which Mr Falconer did not repeat.

"How soon can the two frigates be here?" inquired another.

"In two days, or three at most," was the answer. "But we shall be in no slight danger. I wish we could escape before then."

"No fear about that," answered one of the former speakers. "The Englishmen won't attempt to fight against so over-powering a force, and will, depend on it, haul down their flag as soon as they see the two frigates enter the harbour."

This idea seemed to make the whole party very merry.

Mr Falconer, after sitting quiet for some time, went on deck, and informed the captain of all he had heard.

Captain Podgers was not a little put out by the information he received. He was very unwilling to lose his dollars, but if he remained in harbour, he might lose his ship, and his own life into the bargain; for Mr Falconer did not fail to repeat the threat of the Spaniards, to have him hung up at the yard-arm as a pirate. He vowed that he should be ready to fight one Spanish frigate, but two were more than even the *Dolphin* could venture to tackle.

After pacing the deck two or three times, he summoned the officers into the cabin; and it was finally settled that the other fat friar should be at once sent on shore, with orders to make his appearance next day at noon at the landing-place, with all the dollars that had been collected, and should the amount not be sufficient, he was to warn the inhabitants that their town would be set on fire. That the *Dolphin* might run no risk of being entrapped, she was at once to put to sea, while the boats alone were to go in the following day and bring off the ransom.

The Spaniards were very much alarmed when they saw preparations going on for making sail.

Fortunately, a Spanish merchant among our prisoners spoke a little English, so that Mr Falconer had not to betray to them his knowledge of their language. The fat friar shrugged his shoulders when he heard what he was to do. He seemed, however, not a little pleased to get out of the clutches of the terrible privateersman. As soon as he had been landed, the *Dolphin's* anchor was hove up, and the land breeze still blowing, we sailed out of the harbour.

We were standing on and off the island during the night. It was a calm and beautiful one. I had gone on deck to be near Dick, which I frequently did during his watch, when, the moon shining brightly from behind some light fleecy clouds which floated over the sky, we caught sight of an object gliding over the glittering waters. As it approached, Dick pronounced it to be a raft, with a small square sail set, and soon afterwards we distinguished two figures on it. He hailed. There came, in reply, a faint cry across the water. Directly afterwards the sail was lowered. Mr Falconer, who was officer of the watch, ordered the ship to be hove-to and a boat lowered, which quickly towed the raft and its occupants alongside. The men were hoisted on deck, for they were too weak to climb up by themselves. Dick and I, who had good reason to feel for them, hurried to the gangway. Dick, without asking questions, filled a cup of water and brought it to them; they both drank eagerly.

Mr Falconer while by his orders a couple of hammocks were being got ready for them, inquired who they were and whence they had come. One, who appeared the least exhausted, answered that they had been ten days at sea, and for the three last they had been without food or water, with the exception of half a biscuit apiece, and that they were the survivors of six who had embarked on the raft.

"I am the second mate of the *Juno*, armed whaler," continued the speaker. "Our crew mutinied, murdered the captain and several of the other officers; but the third mate and I, with four men who refused to join them, were turned adrift on this wretched raft, with but a scanty allowance of water and provisions, which the mutineers gave us, asserting that it was enough to support us till we could reach the shore. Calms and light winds prevailed, and we were almost abandoning hope, when, this afternoon, we made the land, though I doubt if we should have survived had we not fallen in with you."

Mr Falconer treated the two mates with great kindness, and did his best to make them comfortable, not doubting the truth of their story. They had farther added, that as soon as they had been sent off from the side of the ship, the mutineers hoisted the black flag, with three cheers, announcing that they intended to turn pirates and attack ships of all nations.

From their account, there remained no doubt that the *Juno* was the ship which had lately engaged the *Dolphin*, and met with so awful, though well-deserved a fate. They also told us that the *Juno* had been about to enter a harbour a short distance off, when two men-of-war were seen, with their lower masts only standing, that several boats had been sent out in chase of the ship, but, a breeze springing up, she had escaped.

This confirmed what Mr Falconer had heard from the Spaniards, and made the captain thankful that he had listened to his advice.

The next day we stood in to the mouth of the harbour, when the boats were sent on shore, each carrying half a dozen torches. Our prisoners were in a great fright on seeing this, saying that the friars would very probably be unable to collect the money, and earnestly urging that we would remain two or three days longer at anchor before setting fire to the town.

"We are not to be so caught, seignors," answered the captain, laughing grimly. "If your friends bring the dollars, well and good; if not, we will make a bonfire which will light the two frigates you expect into the harbour."

Away the boats pulled, one only being left alongside, in which the governor and his companions were ordered to seat themselves. We waited anxiously for some time, when wreaths of smoke were seen to ascend from various parts of the town, and the whole place was shortly in a blaze. The captain considered himself very humane, when he allowed his prisoners, after having been stripped of nearly every particle of clothing, to be put on shore on the nearest point. This he did to revenge himself for the loss of the expected dollars, which he knew, on seeing the town set on fire, had not been obtained.

Scarcely had the boats returned and been hoisted up, when two large ships were seen steering for the entrance of the harbour. Every stitch of canvas the *Dolphin* could carry was set. The strangers, on seeing her, made all sail in chase, and, from the way that they overhauled her, there appeared but little prospect of her escape.

W. H. G. Kingston

CHAPTER TWELVE

MR. NEWTON

The frigates continued to gain on the *Dolphin*. Captain Podgers was in a great state of agitation, dreading the punishment which the Spaniards would justly inflict on us for the injuries we had done them, especially when they found on board the articles we had carried away from the church. "If there was only one of them, I would fight her gladly, and, big as she is, we would beat her, too," exclaimed the captain, as he paced the deck, eyeing the enemy through his spy-glass; and, to do him justice, he was a brave man and not a bad sailor, although he had few other good qualities.

Miss Kitty looked very pale, not from fear of herself, but she dreaded the danger to which those on deck would be exposed.

The wind increased and the sea got up: still we carried on, though our masts and spars bent and cracked. The sails were wetted—hammocks were slung, and men with shot got into them—indeed, every device was used to increase the speed of the ship. After a time, we appeared to be holding our own, if not drawing a little ahead of the enemy.

As evening approached, the wind dropped, and we could see

the sails of the frigates hanging against the masts. Ours soon afterwards collapsed, and we lay perfectly becalmed. Some of the men forward expressed their opinion that the Spaniards would attack as with their boats.

"Little fear of that," said Dick; "they know us too well to wish to come to close quarters. We should have a much better chance of taking them, if we were to try it. I don't know if the captain will think of doing that."

Darkness now came down upon us and shut out the enemy from sight. The captain might have expected an attack to be made on us by the frigates' boats, for he ordered a bright look-out to be kept. Boarding-netting was triced up; the men wore their cutlasses at their sides and pistols in their belts, and pikes were placed ready for use.

Miss Kitty had come on deck, and, seeing me at a little distance, called me to her.

"If there is to be more of that dreadful work, you must come and stay with me, Charley, as before," she said. "I cannot let you risk your young life; you must promise me now."

I did so, though unwillingly.

"When will this fearful fighting end?" she said, sighing. "Though men seem to delight in it, I am sure that it is against all Divine laws, and brings misery and suffering to both parties."

"I hope that we shall escape fighting this time," I observed; "for Dick says that he is sure the Spaniards will not attack us. Perhaps before the morning we shall be able to get away from them."

No one turned in that night, and the crew were kept at their quarters, to be ready for a sudden attack.

When the sun rose out of the ocean, his beams fell on the tails of our foes, throwing a ruddy glow on the calm waters, which shone like a plain of molten gold. Eager eyes were looking out for a breeze. Should it come from the direction of our foes, they would have every chance of catching us; but if ahead, we should have the advantage of them, and thus be able to slip out of their way.

Several hours passed by. We were still the same distance as before from the enemy.

I was on the forecastle with Dick, when I caught sight of a slight ripple which played over the surface. I pointed it out to my companion.

"All right, Charley," he said. "Those catspaws are a good sign. There's another and another."

Presently the sails gave a flap. In a moment every one was in activity: the yards were braced sharp up, the royals filled, then the topgallantsails and topsails bulged out, and away we glided. Looking astern, we saw that the Spaniards still remained becalmed. The captain's ruddy countenance beamed with satisfaction at the hopes of carrying off his booty in safety.

"We shall give the Dons the 'good-bye,'" he shouted out to his wife below.

Kitty quickly came on deck, and I saw how thankful she felt.

Gradually our enemies' sails sank beneath the horizon, and at length we had the satisfaction of losing sight of them altogether. Still the captain observed, that as they would guess the course we had taken, they might be after us; and until two days had passed by, he did not feel altogether secure.

We now steered back to the whaling-ground, where we remained for a couple of months, half filling the ship with oil.

After this we touched at two of the Society Islands. At one of them we saw, as we came to an anchor at some little distance from the beach, beneath a grove of cocoa-nut trees, a neat white cottage built in the English style, with two larger edifices near it, and Dick remarked that one of them looked very like a chapel. The numerous natives, who came off in their canoes, bringing fruits, and vegetables, and fish, were dressed in shirts and trousers, and all behaved in a quiet, orderly way. Two or three of those who came on board spoke English.

"Why, what has come over you people? You are very different sort of fellows to what you were a few years ago, when I was here," observed the captain.

"We were then heathen savages; we are now Christian men," was the answer. "There is our chapel, and there is our school-house; in yonder cottage lives our good pastor, the missionary, Mr Newton, and he will be very glad to receive any who like to visit him."

"I have no fancy for those sort of fellows," growled the captain; "they spoil trade, and prevent our men enjoying their freedom on shore."

Kitty, however, on hearing the account given by the natives, expressed her wish to go and pay a visit to the missionary, and Mr Falconer offered to convey her on shore. The captain could not refuse his request for a boat, though he granted it with an ill grace. Dick was ordered to get one ready. Kitty desired to take me with her, and we were soon walking up a neat pathway towards the cottage.

How beautiful and quiet it looked—everything seemed smiling around.

A gentleman, whom we at once guessed was Mr Newton, appeared at the garden-gate, and cordially invited us into his house. Before entering, we were joined by his wife, a sweet-looking young woman. I thought that, next to Kitty, she was the most perfect being in the world: for almost since I could recollect, I had seen no other females, except the wild natives of the islands we had visited, besides Mrs Podgers. To her she certainly was a very great contrast.

On entering, Kitty was placed on a sofa by our hostess, who removed her bonnet and shawl, and spoke in the sweetest and kindest manner to her. To my surprise, Kitty suddenly burst out crying.

Mr Newton asked her what was the matter.

"Oh!" she exclaimed, "how peaceful and happy all around appears! Oh, how I should like to remain here!"

Kitty then told her how she was situated. Mrs Newton replied that she should be very glad to receive her, and that she hoped she would assist in the work she was engaged in.

"Indeed, I would pray that I might be able to do so," said Kitty.

Mr Falconer looked agitated—a struggle was going on in his heart.

"I have engaged to serve on board yonder ship—my duty forbids me to quit her," he said, in a husky voice. "Yet you will be far, far better off here, and freer from danger, than on board."

"We must not deceive you," said Mr Newton. "Although the natives around us are Christians, there are still many savage heathens in the island, and many more in the neighbouring islands, and we are liable to be attacked by them. It is our duty to be here, but we are not altogether free from danger."

"I should be thankful to leave Miss Kitty in a place of safety," said Mr Falconer, "but that information alters the advice I might have given."

"I will continue on board, and share the dangers the ship may have to go through," exclaimed Kitty, suddenly. "I am, however, deeply grateful for the kind offer you, my friends, have made to me; and do not suppose that it is because I fear to run the risk you speak of, but," and she looked up at Mr Falconer, "I have another reason, which I must ask you not to press me to name."

I do not know whether the missionary and his wife suspected what that reason was, but they did not again urge Miss Kitty to stay with them.

She and I, however, spent the three days the ship remained in the harbour at the missionary's house, and they were the happiest I could ever remember.

How rough and profane appeared my shipmates when I returned on board. Kitty, too, evidently felt the difference between the quiet abode she had left and the cabin of the *Dolphin*.

The *Dolphin* had been several months at sea, and during the time five or six more whales had been caught, when we touched at the Sandwich Islands, where we took on board ten natives, to assist in navigating her. We had also put into the Gallipagos, to refit. They are the most dreary group of islands I have ever visited, dark rocks rising up everywhere round their coasts, with wild black beaches, and huge tortoises, with legs resembling those of elephants, and serpent-like heads, and long lizard-like guanas crawling over them. As no water was to be procured there, we sailed northward till we came in sight of a beautiful island, with hills rising here and there into the blue sky, covered with the richest tropical vegetation.

Directly after, we brought up in a sheltered bay. A number of large canoes came off to us, filled with natives, the skins of the older chiefs almost black, from the elaborate tattoo marks with which they were covered. Those of the younger people were, however, of a light brown hue, the skins of some indeed being quite fair. The heads of the chiefs were decorated with crowns made of long feathers; they wore long loose cloaks of native cloth over their shoulders, and carried in their hands elaborately carved clubs.

The captain, through one of the Sandwich Islanders who could talk English, told them that his object in coming to this island was to get a supply of water, and to cut some spars to make yards for the ship. They replied in a friendly way that he was welcome to do as he wished, and that they would show him the trees likely to suit his purpose.

A number of them were parading the deck, examining everything they saw. When Kitty appeared, they gazed at her with astonishment, she being the first white woman they had probably ever seen. All the people appeared to be very friendly, and anxious to induce our men to go on shore in order to trade, but there being plenty of work on board, the captain would not allow this. At night the natives took their departure, promising to return the next day.

The following morning, several canoes came round the ship, and the captain proposed landing, to select the trees which he wished to have out down. Mr Falconer asked Miss Kitty whether she would like to go on shore. She answered that she did not like the appearance of the natives, and that, though they might profess to be very friendly, she did not trust them, but that she should be very glad to take a sail in the bay, and to make some sketches of the island from the water, and especially of some picturesque rocks which we had passed when entering. The mate gladly undertook to do as she wished, and ordered a boat, with four of the steadiest men in the ship, who were always ready to obey him, to be got ready.

As they expected to be away for some hours, he put some water and provisions into the boat. The steward, not knowing this, had filled a basket, which he also lowered down to the crew. Mr Falconer had intended that Dick should go, but the first mate had directed him to do some work, which kept him occupied, and had told me to attend on him. I knew that Miss Kitty would gladly have me with her, and felt disappointed when I saw the boat sail away down the harbour. The natives seemed to take little notice of the boat's departure, probably they thought she had gone for a short distance only, and would soon return.

The captain, with the carpenter and his mates, and a boat's crew, now went on shore. Dick and I were at work on the bowsprit, I sitting by him, holding the rope-yarn and grease-pot. As soon as the captain was gone, the natives began to invite our men on shore, and several of them, declaring that it was very hard that they should be kept on board, slipped

W. H. G. Kingston

into the canoes, and allowed the savages to carry them off. Others followed their example. The officers shouted to them to return, but their orders were not attended to. More canoes now came off, full of savages, who, as they got alongside, clambered on board, till the deck was crowded with them, so that the crew who remained at their duty could scarcely move about. The first mate, seeing this, ordered the natives back into their canoes. I had, while the mate was issuing his orders, turned my glance aft, when, at that moment, he cried out to Lieutenant Pyke, who was below, to get his men under arms, and then signed to the natives crowding the deck to return to their canoes. Thinking, apparently, to make the savages understand him better, he incautiously gave a shove to one of the chiefs who was standing near him. The savage, uttering a fearful cry, whirled round his heavy club and struck the poor mate dead on the deck. It was a signal to his followers. In an instant every club was upraised and aimed at the head of the nearest seaman.

Dick, hearing the savages shout, looked up from his work, and seeing what was taking place, laid hold of me by the collar and dragged me along to the jib-boom end, whence we witnessed the dreadful scene enacted on deck.

CHAPTER THIRTEEN

IN THE CLUTCHES OF THE CHIEF

The crew of the *Dolphin*, though numerous and well accustomed to the use of arms, being thus taken unawares, were almost helpless. The sharp-edged war-clubs of the natives came crashing down upon their heads, as they ran here and there in search of weapons to defend themselves. Lieutenant Pyke was struck dead the instant he appeared at the companion-hatch. The second mate was treated in the same way, while the boatswain, with a few men who gathered round him, made a desperate attempt to defend himself; but he and his party were overpowered by numbers, and cut down, after they had killed several of the natives. Some of our men jumped down below, but were followed by the savages. Whether they were killed, or whether any escaped, we could not tell. A few ran up the rigging, where the natives appeared afraid to follow them.

In a few minutes, besides Dick and me, not a white man whom we could see, except those aloft, remained alive. The natives now began dancing frantically about the deck, whirling their clubs over their heads, and shouting at the top of their voices for joy of their victory. They either did not observe Dick and me, or knowing that we must at length come in, did not think us worth their notice. I felt almost

W. H. G. Kingston

overpowered with horror. In spite of that, however, I thought of dear Miss Kitty, dreading that she and Mr Falconer, with those in the boat, would, on their return, have to share the terrible fate of our other companions; while I fully expected Dick and I would soon be summoned off to be killed.

What had become of Mrs Podgers, and those who had been below at the moment of the attack, we could not tell.

"Oh, Dick, what are we to do?" I exclaimed, trembling with fear.

"We must trust to God, Charley," he answered. "He will take care of us, though how that is to be, is more than I can say. I can only hope that the savages, fierce as they are, will not have the heart to kill a little boy like you; and it can matter little what becomes of an old fellow, such as I am. Say your prayers, Charley, though you cannot kneel down. That does not matter."

The savages all this time continued dancing on the deck, as if they would beat it in, shouting at the top of their voices, and flourishing their war-clubs, looking more like a gang of demons let loose than human beings.

"It will be bad enough for us, Charley, even though the natives don't kill and eat us, but my mind is most troubled about poor Miss Kitty. What will become of her, if they get hold of the boat? and there's no chance that I can see of her escaping."

"I was thinking of her, too," I said, "and Mr Falconer. The savages will murder him and the boat's crew, as they have the rest. Oh, Dick! I cannot stand it. I wish they would kill me at once!"

I felt, as I spoke, like the hapless bird fascinated by the glance of the serpent, and could scarcely restrain myself from clambering on board and rushing among the savages.

"Hold fast, Charley," said Dick. "I wish I had not said what I did—you have got your best days before you. If the savages wanted to kill us, they would have done so before now. See, they are growing calmer, and are talking together; they, perhaps, will be satisfied with gaining possession of the ship, and all the plunder in her, and won't kill those who make no resistance."

Soon after Dick had said this, a tall chief with a high plume of feathers on his head, and his almost white skin only slightly tattooed, advanced to the heel of the bowsprit, and, looking towards Dick and me, shouted out some words, and beckoned us to come in.

"What shall we do, Dick?" I asked. "Will he kill me, do you think?"

"There's no help for it, Charley," answered Dick. "But don't be afraid; he shall kill me before he hurts you. Just get round and keep close behind me, and I will ask him to take care of you; he does not look as savage as the rest."

I followed Dick, though I confess my alarm was so great that I could scarcely hold on. As we got to the inner end of the bowsprit, I observed that the chief placed his bloodstained club against the bulwarks; he then lifted up both his hands, to show that they held no weapon. Dick, therefore, advanced more boldly, and getting on deck, still keeping me behind him, confronted the chief.

"I make bold to ask you to let this little chap go free, Mr Savage," said Dick, pointing to me. "He has never done you

W. H. G. Kingston

no harm, and never will. It cannot do you any good if you kill him, and he is so thin, he would make but a poor meal, if you want to eat him."

Although the chief could not have understood a word that Dick said, he seemed to comprehend his meaning, and, putting his hand on his head and mine, he signified that we were his property, and that he would take care of us. He even smiled when he looked at me, and seemed to inquire whether I was Dick's son, so Dick fancied; for he replied, "He is all the same as my child, and if you hurt him, it will be the worse for you." Our friend then called up two other men, who appeared to belong to him as a sort of bodyguard, and then charged them to take care of us, while he went aft and spoke to the other chiefs.

Meantime the natives had begun to hoist up the goods from the hold, and to load their canoes with them, our new friend being apparently engaged in securing his share of the booty. Dick and I were thus left on the forecastle, and could observe what was going on. We often turned our eyes towards the mouth of the harbour, dreading to see the boat return. And yet, what could become of her, with no friendly port near, should she not come back?

A considerable time having passed, the young chief's canoe came round under the bows, and he made signs to us to lower ourselves into her. Just before I did so, I cast my eyes once more seaward, and there I caught sight of a boat's sail. Mr Falconer and Kitty were returning, unsuspicious of the dreadful circumstances which had occurred. How I wished that I could go off and warn them.

We had scarcely thought about the captain and the rest of the men on shore. If they had escaped, we need not have much apprehension about ourselves; but if they had been put to death, we, I still dreaded, on reaching the shore might meet with the same fate.

"What can we do, Dick, to let Miss Kitty and the mate know their danger?" I asked. "If they come up the harbour, there will be no chance for them."

"We can do nothing, Charley," he answered. "They are in God's hands, as we are, and we must trust to Him to take care of us all."

The young chief now made another sign to Dick and me to get into the canoe, so we lowered ourselves down, and went up to where the chief was standing. His canoe, like many others around, was of considerable length, fully forty feet, though not more than a foot and a half wide, and of about the same depth. She was kept from upsetting by outriggers projecting from the bow, middle, and stern, with a long piece of light wood secured to the extremity of each. On the upper part of the stem, which projected about two feet, was a carved head of some animal; while the after part also projected six feet or more beyond the actual stern, something like the shape of a Dutch skate. The paddles were neatly made of a hard black wood, highly polished, with slender handles, and the blades of an oval form. I afterwards examined the canoe, and found that it was composed of many pieces of the bread-fruit tree, cut into planks and sewed together with the fibres of the outside shell of the cocoa-nut. The seams were covered inside and out with strips of bamboo sewed to the edge of each plank, to keep in a stuffing of cocoa-nut fibre. The keel consisted of one piece, which ran the whole length, and was hollowed out in the form of a canoe, being, indeed, the foundation of the vessel. Three pieces of thick plank, placed as partitions, divided the interior into four parts, and served for timbers to keep her from separating or closing together. She had also a mat sail, broad at the top, and narrowing to a point at the foot.

The chief told as to sit down, and directed his crew to paddle towards the shore. This they did, accompanied by several other canoes, which were apparently under his command.

We frequently turned our eyes towards the boat, but the wind was scant and light, and she made but little progress up the harbour. Probably Miss Kitty and the mate were in no hurry to return on board. The men who had escaped up the rigging were still there; but whether the captain's wife and those who had fled below had survived the massacre we could not tell. The ship was still crowded with savages, who were busily employed carrying up what they could find below and had strength to remove. The oil-casks must, however, have been beyond their power to lift, though Dick observed that they would be sure to try and get hold of the iron hoops, and be rather astonished when the oil burst out over them.

Our captor directed his course towards a small inner bay, on the shores of which were several huts, where we concluded that he lived. Though some of his men cast savage glances at us, and looked as if they would like to knock out our brains, we were not ill-treated, nor was anything taken from us.

On landing, we were allowed to remain by ourselves while the crews of the canoes were busy in unloading them as fast as they could.

There was close at hand, forming one side of the little bay, a high rock, whence Dick thought that we could get a good sight of the whole harbour. We set off, and, unnoticed by the busy natives, made our way to the top of it. We were not disappointed in our expectations, and from it could see both the ship and the boat. The latter had made but little way, and, finding the wind against her, had lowered her sail and taken to the oars. More canoes were collecting alongside, and we concluded that the chief and his followers were going to return for a further supply of booty. We were allowed to remain on the rocks, the natives probably knowing that we could not make our escape.

The wind after a time freshened a little, and the boat was drawing nearer. As we were looking towards her, a loud report reached our ears, and, turning our eyes towards the ship, we saw the masts and deck rising upwards, surrounded by a dense smoke, and a thick mass of the shattered fragments of numberless articles, mingled with the boom-boats, companion-hatch, caboose, and human beings mangled and torn. For a few seconds they seemed to hang in the air, and then were scattered far and wide around the ship. The masts falling into the water, crushed several of the canoes alongside, and the shrieks and cries of the natives, who had escaped with life, while they paddled away in dismay, came over the waters towards us.

Dick and I held our breath, and I saw horror depicted in his countenance.

"Though the savages deserve what they have got, it may be the worse for us," he muttered. "They will now knock us on the head, to a certainty."

I made no reply, but I feared that what Dick said would prove true.

Flames now burst out from the ship, and several guns which were loaded went off, sending their shot flying among the natives, and creating still further dismay.

So absorbed were we for some minutes in watching the ship, that we had almost forgotten the boat. Again looking towards her, I saw that her sail was hoisted, and that she was running before the wind towards the harbour's mouth.

"Mr Falconer guesses what has happened; I am sure of that," said Dick, "and he would rather trust to carrying Miss Kitty off into the wide ocean than to the mercy of the savages, though I am afraid they will have a hard time of it, even if they get clear."

"Oh, Dick!" I cried out, "see, there are some of the savages after them, and they may be overtaken."

Such, indeed, was the case. Several canoes which at the time of the explosion had been at a distance from the ship, watching, apparently, the approaching boat, on seeing her standing seaward, began to paddle after her. Though they had no sails, they glided rapidly over the water, and there seemed but little probability that our friends would effect their escape.

CHAPTER FOURTEEN

MOTAKEE

So absorbed were Dick and I in watching the boat with Miss Kitty on board and the savages pursuing them, that we did not think of ourselves or the fate which too probably awaited us. The savages paddled with might and main, resolved, it seemed, to revenge on our friends the destruction which had overtaken so many of their people. They were gaining rapidly on the boat, though her crew were pulling hard at the oars. I felt inclined to cry with agitation as I thought of what Miss Kitty would have to endure, when the boat's sail filled out, and a freshening breeze carried her along faster than she had hitherto been moving. The wind still further increased. Away she shot ahead, distancing her pursuers. She gained the harbour's mouth, and, steering out to sea, ran on till her white sail appeared a mere speck in the horizon; while the savages, disappointed of their prey, paddled back towards the shore.

Meantime the ill-fated *Dolphin* continued burning, and was now in flames fore and aft, the savages having been too much alarmed to make any attempt to extinguish the fire. The men who had been aloft had clung to the mast when it fell, though we could scarcely hope that they had escaped uninjured. We saw, however, that several of them were still hanging on to it, while it floated free of the burning ship. The natives, on discovering them, approached the mast, and dragged them into their canoes. What they intended to do with them we could not tell, but we feared that they would murder them, as we supposed they also would us.

The young chief who had taken possession of us had not reached the ship when she blew up, and we now saw him and his people landing in the little bay above which we were seated. We had made no attempt to conceal ourselves. He beckoned to us to come down.

"We must put a bold face on the matter," said Dick, taking my hand. "Cheer up, Charley. I don't think he intends to hurt you; and if he kills me, remember, do your best to escape, and don't turn into a savage, as they are sure to try and make you, and cover you all over with tattoo marks."

"Oh, they must not kill you, Dick; they sha'n't kill you!" I cried out. "I will let them kill me first."

I felt, indeed, that I would much rather be put to death than see my kind friend murdered before my eyes.

Dick, leading me by the hand, approached the chief, whose club I expected every moment to see upraised to strike us dead. Instead of doing so, however, looking at me kindly, he took me by the hand and made a speech to Dick, which we, of course, could not understand, but which, from its tone, relieved us somewhat from our apprehensions. I afterwards discovered that it was to the effect that he had promised to befriend us; and knowing that the destruction of the ship and the death of his people was not owing to as, that would not alter his purpose.

"Thank you kindly, sir," said Dick, touching his hat

sailor-fashion. "If you will treat this boy well, it's all I care for. I speak him fair, Charley, for your sake," he said to me, "and by the cut of his jib, I think he will be as good as his word."

The chief, whose name we found was Motakee, or "The good-looking one," now addressed his people, who had been casting somewhat threatening glances at us, and, I suspect, had we been left to their tender mercies, would very soon have knocked us on the head. Our new friend having appointed several of his people to guard us, told us to follow him along the shore. After going a short distance, we reached another much larger beach, on which a number of canoes were drawn up and a large concourse of people assembled. We looked about for the captain and our shipmates, who had at first landed. On going a little farther, what was our horror to see the greater number of them lying dead on the shore, with their heads so battered that we could scarcely recognise them. We knew the captain, however, by his figure and dress; we had, therefore, too much reason to suppose that we were the only survivors of the *Dolphin's* crew, with the exception of those who had escaped in the boat and the men who had been saved on the mast. We saw the latter alive in some of the canoes still afloat. Whether the captain had been killed before the destruction of the ship, we could not at first ascertain, but I believe he and the rest were murdered after the accident.

The chief held a long consultation, while Dick and I stood at a little distance watching them, uncertain what was to be our fate.

"Cheer up, Charley," said Dick. "I would fight for you as long as there's life in me, if it would be of any use; but I don't think, savages as they are, that they will have the heart to kill you; and as for me, as I said before, they may do as they like, though I wish I was sure they would not eat me afterwards."

"Oh, Dick, Dick!" I cried out, "don't think of anything so horrid! I will ask the young chief not to hurt you, and I will tell him he had better kill me first."

Just then the consultation came to an end, and Motakee, coming up to us, made signs that we need not be afraid, and that he would protect us.

I afterwards found, when I came to know their language, that he had told the other chiefs that on seeing me he had been reminded of a little boy he had lost, and that he had saved Dick on my account, supposing that he was my father, or, at all events, my friend.

Six men, one of whom was a Sandwich Islander, named Tui, who had been saved on the mast, were now brought on shore. As we watched them, we fully believed that the savages would put them to death, as they had the other poor fellows. Tui, however, stepped forward and addressed the natives in a language which they appeared to comprehend. They again consulted together, the unhappy men standing apart, uncertain whether they might not at any moment find the clubs of the savages crashing through their brains. Trusting to Motakee's protection, I felt inclined to rush forward and plead for them, but Dick held me back.

"You will do no good, Charley," he said, "and one of those savages may in a moment give you a tap with his club, and kill you, as an idle boy does a fly."

The five poor fellows stood collected together, looking pale as death, but they were as brave as any of the men on board. Among them I recognised Tom Clode, the armourer, and Mat Davis, the carpenter's mate.

The discussion seemed to last a very long time. Tui was listened to attentively, as he every now and then put in a word. At length five of the principal chiefs rose from their mats, and, stepping forward, each put his hand on one of the men. At first I thought they were going to kill them, as they led them away; but Tui, coming up, told us that they were only going to be taken as slaves. Another old chief now advanced and put his hand on Dick's shoulder.

"He going take you for slave," said Tui.

"I have no wish to be idle, but I would rather have chosen a master with a better-looking mug of his own," observed Dick. "I hope the old gentleman lives not far from your friend, Charley; for I can't stand being separated from you."

I burst into tears as Dick said this, when Motakee, coming up, tried, in a gentle way, to soothe me.

"He is a good young fellow, that he is," cried Dick; "and as you are likely to be well off with him, it's little odds what happens to me."

Motakee, finding that my tears continued to flow, endeavoured to persuade the old chief, Toobo Cava, to allow Dick to continue with him. This, however, he refused, and replied that he might rather allow me to accompany Dick. Tui told us what was said.

"I would like to have you, Charley," said Dick, "but you will be much better off with Motakee, and, indeed, I doubt if he would let you come, however much you may wish it."

Dick was right; for after another long palaver, Motakee took me by the hand, while old Toobo Cava led off Dick.

"Keep up your spirits, Charley, and don't forget the lessons I have taught you; say your prayers, and be a good boy," cried Dick, looking back towards me. "We will manage to see each other, or these talking fellows are cleverer than I take them to be."

Motakee, accompanied by his people, conducted me back to the bay where we had landed, and thence to his house, which was situated in a valley but a short distance from the shore. It stood on a platform of large stones, nearly twelve feet above the ground, and was fully thirty feet in length, though considerably narrower. The back of the house was fourteen feet in height, the roof sloping down towards the front, which was scarcely more than five feet high, but the walls were of a uniform height all round, thus the farther part of the house between them and the roof was entirely open. The front part, into which we first entered by a very small door, had a floor composed of the rough stones of the platform, but the inner part, separated from it by a partition, was covered with fine mats. At one end was the bed-place, which consisted of two horizontal poles, about a foot from the ground, with matting stretched between them. On this the chief and his family reclined, resting their heads on one of the poles, which served as a pillow, while their feet extended towards the other. Around the walls, which were also composed of matting, were hung numerous weapons, spears, clubs, axes, slings, and stilts, on which I found that the people were very fond of walking.

These stilts are elaborately carved poles, with carved figures towards the lower end, on the heads of which the feet rest. The chief took down a pair, and, to amuse me, mounted on them, and ran over the ground with great rapidity, now standing on one leg, now on the other, and twirling round and performing all sorts of extraordinary feats. He having set the example, others followed it, till nearly all the men and the boys in the village turned out on stilts, and began chasing each other over the rough ground, as much at home as if they were treading it with their feet, instead of being mounted high above it.

The sports being over, Motakee led me to the farther end of the village, where there was a sort of temple. In front of the temple were a number of little buildings a couple of feet high, on each of which stood a carved figure, surrounded with shells, and feathers, and whales' teeth. He and his people sat down before them, and bowed, and uttered certain words, and then bowed again, leading me to suppose that they were performing some religious ceremony.

Having finished his prayers, if such all this bowing and muttering words could be intended for, the chief conducted me back to his house. Here he introduced me to his wife, pretty-looking young woman, of a bright brown colour, clothed in somewhat scanty garments, composed of cloth, manufactured from the paper-mulberry tree. She received me very kindly, and we sat down to a supper consisting of fish, and various roots, and other vegetables and fruits.

I had till now been under the dreadful impression that the people were cannibals; but there was nothing in the repast set before me which made me unwilling to partake of it. On the contrary, as I was very hungry, I set to with a will, and the people standing round seemed pleased at seeing me eat with so good an appetite.

Several days passed by; the chief and his wife seemed to consider that I had taken the place of their lost child, and treated me as such with much kindness. I had, however, neither seen nor heard anything of Dick, and I gave Motakee to understand that I wished to go out and look for him, to which he, by signs, replied that it would be dangerous for me to wander about by myself, as the people of other tribes might kill me, and that I must remain quietly where I was.

I remembered Dick's plan of keeping time when we were in our solitary island, and I cut a stick, on which I marked the days of the week. I did not forget either his parting advice to me, and every night and morning I knelt down and said my prayers. The natives understood what I was about, and never interrupted me, and treated me with more respect than even some of the men did on board the *Dolphin*.

At the end of a couple of months I saw that something unusual was taking place in the village. The men were polishing up their arms, and the women were engaged in making baskets and cooking provisions. This led me to suppose that an expedition of some sort was about to take place.

Motakee called me to him one day, and told me by signs that he was going away, and that he would place me under charge of some one who would take good care of me during his absence. I told him that I should be very sorry to be parted from him, and asked him to let me go, hoping that by some means I might hear of Dick. He shook his head, and told me that as danger would have to be encountered, I was too young as yet, but that when I grew older, he would teach me the use of the native weapons, and allow me to accompany him to war. He then led me to another house, somewhat smaller than his own, in which the principal inmate was an old woman. Though Moola—that was her name—was very old and dry and withered, from the expression of her countenance and the way in which he treated her, I was led to suppose that she was Motakee's mother. Such, indeed, was the case. She spoke kindly to me, and I had no reason to fear that I should be ill-treated.

After this Motakee led out his people, all armed with clubs, and hatchets, and spears; the heads of the principal men being decorated with plumes of feathers, but, with the exception of cloths round their waists, entirely destitute of clothing. From this I knew that they were about to proceed on some warlike expedition, and, though they felt confident of success, I could not help remembering that they might be defeated; and should they be so, what would become of me? Again I asked the chief if he could give me any information about Dick? My heart sank within me; for, from the reply he made, he led me to suppose that some accident had happened to my faithful friend.

W. H. G. Kingston

CHAPTER FIFTEEN

MOOLA

Old Moola kept a watchful eye on me, as if she divined my intention of trying to make my escape to go in search of Dick on the first opportunity which might occur.

I concluded that if the warriors were away he would be less carefully looked after than usual, and would try to find me; for I was very sure that he was as anxious about me as I was about him.

There were a good many other boys in the village, and I used to play with them, and did my best to excel them in all their sports. I found, after some practice, that I could walk on stilts as well as they could. I induced them to run races, and I very frequently came off the victor. They had an advantage, from being more lightly clad than I was, that is to say, while I wore my shirt and trousers, they had no clothing whatever.

The women, meantime, were employed in their usual domestic occupations, in making cloth by beating out the bark of the paper-mulberry tree, and manufacturing mats and baskets. I afterwards observed that they were always employed in such occupations, while the men, when at home, cultivated the fields, and caught fish with nets and fish-hooks, the latter formed of mother-of-pearl, as also with bone, and wooden harpoons. Besides the articles I have mentioned, they make calabashes from gourds, and kava-cups formed of the cocoa-nut, as also cradles for their children, hollowed out of a log with great neatness. They also use small chests, which are in like manner hollowed out of solid pieces of wood, with covers to them, and wooden bowls and stands, on which various objects are hung out of the way of the rats. Those animals are great pests, and to preserve their more valuable articles, the natives suspend them in baskets from the roofs of their houses, by lines passing through the bottoms of inverted calabashes, so that, should the creatures reach the polished surface of the calabashes, they slip off on to the ground, without being able to climb beneath them.

Moola's house was furnished with all the articles I have mentioned, supplied to her by the people of her tribe, who looked up to her with great respect. As I was under her charge, and was moreover regarded in the light of a chief's son, no one interfered with me, or questioned what I thought fit to do. This was a great advantage, and I hoped would enable me to carry out my plan. Besides my amusements on shore, I soon learned to swim and to paddle a canoe, and other boys and I used frequently to go out in the bay. It occurred to me that, by gradually extending our excursions, I might be able to get along the shore to some distance, and there land and make my way into the interior. To do this, however, I found that I should require two or more companions, and they might not be disposed to assist me. I became expert in fishing with the line and hooks and in spearing fish, but I could not manage to dive in the way the natives did. Some of them, with a hoop-net in one hand, and a stick in the other, would dart down into the deep water among the coral, and with the stick drive the fish hidden among its recesses into the net. This operation was not unattended with danger. Sharks were constantly prowling about, to snap up a person unprepared for their attacks; and one day, a young man who, according to custom, wore his hair loose, was caught by it among the coral, and, unable to extricate himself, was drowned before his companions could go to his assistance. When the sea rolled in a heavy surf on the shore, it was common amusement for boys, and even for girls, to paddle out on little rafts, mounting to the top of the surf, and if the raft was upset, which frequently happened, they would dive under the sea, and come up again on the other side.

Besides these amusements, in which I took a part, I tried to learn some of the arts practised by the natives. I never found the time hang heavily on my hands, still I was continually thinking how I could manage to find Dick. After considering the matter, I abandoned the idea of making the attempt by water, and resolved to try and escape by land. Fearing that the warriors would return, I determined to put it into execution without delay. I had secreted as much food in the pockets of my jacket as they could hold, and, late in the day, I challenged my companions to a race on stilts across the country, pointing to a rock which projected from the hillside at some distance. They laughed at me when they saw me dressed in my jacket, declaring that I should have no chance, and willingly agreed to give me a short start, believing that, encumbered as I was, they could easily come up with me. Old Moola, not suspecting my intentions, came out from her hut, and promised to reward the victor. We took our places, and away we started. I exerted myself to the utmost to keep ahead of my competitors, and found, as I had hoped, that I was at first gaining on them rapidly, although they in the end, I have no doubt, would have overtaken me. As soon as I felt sure that I was well out of sight, hidden by a ridge over which I had passed, I turned off to the right, and ran on along the valley, where the even ground allowed me to continue at a good speed. I then, turning into a wood, jumped off my stilts, and, having concealed them among the hushes, continued my flight on foot. I went on and on, avoiding cultivated land or any huts where I might meet with inhabitants, till the increasing darkness compelled me to stop. I had no dread of wild beasts or venomous snakes, as I knew the island was free from them. I could therefore lie down on the dry grass, and recover my strength without fear; and I hoped that the other boys would make their way to the goal, and not think of looking for me till the darkness prevented them from doing so.

I slept soundly, and soon after I awoke the first streaks of dawn appeared in the sky. Having taken a little food, and drank some water from a rivulet which flowed by, I proceeded onwards, intending to lie in wait near the first village I should come to, in the hopes that one or other of the captive Englishmen might be there, and might give me information about Dick, should he himself not appear.

I went on for some way, keeping myself concealed as much as possible among the trees, till I saw several native huts before me, just on the borders of a wood. Making my way through the wood, I discovered a tree which I could climb. I managed, not without difficulty, to get up it, and, when near the top, concealed by the leafy boughs, I could survey all that went on in the village below me. The people at length began to come out of their huts, but I saw only women, or old men and boys, showing that the fighting part of the population had not returned. In vain I watched for Dick, or one of the other white men. Disappointed at not seeing them, I descended from my perch, afraid that some of the people might come into the wood and discover me. Hurrying on, I had got to no great distance, when I heard voices from among the trees behind me, showing that, had I not escaped when I did, I should have been found out.

W. H. G. Kingston

I could by this time speak the native language quite well enough to make myself understood, and I resolved, should I meet any one, to go up and speak with confidence, as if I had full right to be at liberty.

In a short time I reached another village. Here I watched as before, but though several natives were moving about, none of my shipmates were to be seen, and the dreadful idea occurred to me that they had all been murdered. My heart sank, still I determined to continue my search.

The direct path from village to village was very much shorter than the road I was compelled to take, as I had to make wide circuits to avoid observation. I was now at a considerable distance from Motakee's village, and I hoped, even should I be seen by any of the natives, there was not much risk of being sent back. This made me less cautious than before. Feeling thirsty, I had gone to a bright spring which gushed out of a rock, to drink, when, on looking up, I saw a young girl with several gourds, which she had brought to fill with water. She cast an astonished glance at me, and inquired where I had come from. I told her at once that I knew from her looks she was kind, and could only wish to do me good; that I had belonged to the ship which had been taken by her people, and that I was in search of my guardian. "I have not mistaken you," I added; "you will help me, if you can?"

She looked pleased, and replied that she could feel for me, away from my country and friends, and that she certainly would not betray me. She added that she had heard that there was an Englishman living in the next village, kept a prisoner by an old chief who ruled there, who was very stern and cruel, and made him work very hard, and that he had become very ill.

"The chief himself has gone away to fight, and you will have less difficulty in seeing your countryman than would have been the case had he been at home."

I thanked the young girl very much for her information, and she having pointed out the road I was to take, I proceeded on my journey. I went on till I came to the village. I could easily distinguish the chief's house, which was considerably larger than that of the other natives. Some short distance from it was a small hut. It was built in a different fashion to that of the natives, and not so neatly put together. On one side was a garden, apparently lately formed, and carefully cultivated. It struck me at once that it must be the work of an Englishman. I concealed myself, as before, so that I could watch the proceedings of the inhabitants. After a time, I saw a woman, with a basket in her hand, approach the hut: she looked cautiously round, to ascertain, apparently, that no one was watching her, and then went in. She was old, and far from comely, but, even at the distance she was from me, her countenance looked kind and gentle. She soon came out again, looking about as before, and hurrying away. I observed that her basket was empty. This convinced me that she had been to take provisions to the inmate of the hut, whoever he might be. I determined to ascertain this.

"May I come in," I asked, in the native language.

"Who's there?" was the reply, in English.

I knew the voice; it was Dick's.

He lay on a bed formed of dry grass and mats; I hurried up to him.

"I have found you at last, my dear, dear Dick!" I exclaimed.

"Charley, is it you, yourself? Then you are not dead," he

cried out. "I was told you were, and it well-nigh broke my heart. I shall get well now though. Where have you been? what have you been about?"

I soon told him, and how I had managed to elude my captors. He expressed his delight that I had not been ill-treated, as he had been.

"That old chief is a regular tyrant; he made me work for him till I could work no longer, and then would have let me die of starvation, if a good woman had not, at the risk of her life, brought me food. Bless them! they are all alike, black and white, when a fellow is in trouble, however bad they may be in other respects. Things were not so bad at first. Tui, who lives not far off, came over with Mat Davis, and helped me to put up this hut; or otherwise, as far as my old master was concerned, I should have had to sleep out of doors. He, however, would not let them come again, and I have had to look out for myself. The only pleasant thing that has happened to me was seeing Toobo Cava go off to the war, but he will be back again soon, I fear, and then the hard work will begin once more. But you must not stay here, Charley; I don't know what he would do if he caught you, though it will be a sore grief to me to have you separated from me."

I told Dick that I was determined at all hazards to stay with him.

"We will argue the point, Charley," said Dick.

He at last allowed me to remain till the following day. He had been so well supplied with food, that he was able to give me as much as I required. I spent half the night sitting up talking to him, and had the satisfaction of seeing that my visit was doing him good, his complaint being more the result of anxiety and ill-treatment than anything else.

"I scarcely know what to advise you to do, Charley," he said. "If you are caught here, you may be hardly dealt with, and yet I don't like to tell you to leave me; though, as you say the people you have been living with have treated you well, it will be best for you to make your way back to them."

"Come what will, I am not going to run away and leave you while you are sick and helpless," I answered. "God will take care of me if I ask Him; you have often told me that, and so I will say my prayers and go to sleep."

I did so, and coiled myself away on a heap of grass by Dick's side.

The next morning we were awoken by hearing a great noise in the village. We found that we had both overslept ourselves. Dick went to the door of the hut, to ascertain the cause of the hubbub, telling me to keep concealed under the mats. After some time he came back.

"I guessed how it is," he said; "the fighting men have returned from the war, but, as far as I can discover, the old chief is not among them. He has, I suspect, been knocked on the head, and serve him right too. They are mourning for him, it seems, and it will be as well to keep out of their way, lest they take it into their heads to sacrifice us to his ghost, as I know is the fashion among these savages."

Dick spoke quite coolly, but our danger was great. He again told me to keep snug under the mats, and I saw him walking up and down the hut, evidently very unhappy. "I don't care for myself," I heard him say. "Poor dear Charley, I wish that he was out of the scrape. Well, well; we have been saved before, and we may be saved again. It's a great thing to know that God looks after us poor fellows better than we can look after ourselves." While he was speaking, the noise increased.

W. H. G. Kingston

Never did I hear such savage shrieks, cries, and howls.

"The people are cutting themselves with knives, and flints, and spear-heads, to show their grief for their dead chief," observed Dick, after he had taken another look outside the hut. He sat down, and seemed considering what he should do. After some time, I heard a footstep approaching the hut, and the old woman I had before seen entered.

She looked very anxious, and told Dick he must get out of the way, and hide himself for some days, when he would be safe. Dick thanked her warmly.

"You have been kind to me, and you will be kind, I know, to my son; and if you will hide us away together I shall be happy."

Dick then told me to come forward. The old woman looked very much surprised at seeing me, and on hearing that I had been taken care of by Motakee, advised me to go back at once to him, and to take Dick along with me. There was no time to be lost. Having ascertained that the coast was clear, she told us to hurry off into the wood, and to make our way as fast as we could to Motakee's village, promising, if she could, to put her people on a wrong scent, should they think of pursuing us.

We did as she had advised. We had not, however, got far into the wood, when, as we were making our way along the hillside, as I looked back through an opening in the trees, I saw a number of people advancing towards the hut, shrieking, and shouting, and flourishing their weapons. There could be little doubt that their intention was to get hold of Dick. We hurried on, and did not stop till we were far away beyond the sound of their voices.

CHAPTER SIXTEEN

DICK AND CHARLEY REUNITED

The natives in the villages were so busy celebrating their victory, or mourning for their slain warriors, that Dick and I escaped observation and reached the spot where I had left my stilts.

"Now, Dick," said I, mounting on them, "come along; you shall hide near the village, and I will go boldly into it, as if I had been taking only a longer walk than usual. Then, as Motakee will be glad to see me back, I will tell him that the other old chief, Toobo Cava, is dead, and you ought to be set at liberty, and ask him to protect you. If he says he cannot, you must make your escape, and I'll follow; but if he says yes, we will live together happily till we can get away from this savage country."

Dick agreed to my plan. As we got near the village, I left him, hid away in the wood, and stalked forward on my stilts.

I saw Motakee haranguing the people, and recounting his exploits, so I at once advanced and saluted him, as if I had no reason to be ashamed of anything I had done. He did not look angry, but told me he was happy to see me. The boys shouted, and asked where I had been.

W. H. G. Kingston

"I told you I should beat you," I answered; "and I took a somewhat longer run than any of you, I've a notion. When shall you be ready for another race?"

"We will beat you next time, though," they cried out, not putting any further inconvenient questions to me.

My appearance had somewhat disturbed the usual formality of the meeting, and the chief, having commanded silence, went on with his speech.

As soon as it was over, I descended from my stilts, and begged him to grant the petition I had to make. I praised Dick as he had deserved, and told the chief all he had done for me; and, to my great joy, he replied that he would protect him, as, his owner being dead, no one else could claim his services.

On this I hurried off and brought in Dick, who was well received by the people. I afterwards told the chief the trick I had played, at which he was very much amused.

Dick at once set to work to make himself useful, and soon gained Motakee's confidence, so that he allowed us both to roam about as we chose.

The victory gained by our friends over the Typees, the tribe they had attacked, had put them in excellent humour. They had burned down their villages, destroyed their fruit trees, and carried off their canoes. The slaughter had been, we were sorry to hear, considerable on both sides; for the Typees possessed several strong forts, formed of large stones and huge pieces of timber. These had been taken by assault, when all within had been put to the sword. Dick said he was surprised that savages could construct such strong works, for it would have proved a tough job, even to English sailors, to take some of those he had seen.

Months and months passed by, and yet no vessel had come near the island, in which we might make our escape. The people had got, we suspected, a bad name; for the *Dolphin* was not the only vessel, we found, they had cut off, while they had attempted unsuccessfully to capture several others. Our only hope was that a man-of-war would come in, which might carry us off by force, should the natives refuse to give us up.

The chief, who had adopted me as his son, seemed determined not to let me go, and I found that I was narrowly watched wherever I wandered.

Dick managed, at length, to communicate with some of the other men; though one or two were content to remain among the natives, having married and adopted their customs: the rest expressed an earnest wish to escape.

A tremendous storm having occurred, when it seemed as if the whole island would be carried away by the fury of the waves, the wreck of the *Dolphin* was cast up on the beach.

Dick told me that Mat Davis had long been thinking of building a vessel, and that the carpenter's tools having been among the first things landed, he hoped, if he could get hold of them, to be able to build a craft which would convey us to the coast of South America. He had persuaded the chiefs, that if they could have such a vessel as he described, they might not only overpower all the neighbouring tribes, but sail in quest of foreign lands, which they might conquer. The chiefs listened eagerly to this proposal, and promised to assist him in carrying out his undertaking.

Mat Davis, who was a clever fellow, was the chief architect.

Assisted by the armourer, a forge was put up for the ironwork, and he set the natives to cut down trees and hew out timbers and planks. Others were employed in rope-making and in manufacturing fine matting for the sails, as all the *Dolphin's* canvas had been burnt. Dick and I were allowed to lend a hand, but as, with the exception of Davis and Clode, all were unskilled, the work proceeded but slowly. The hopes of escaping encouraged the Englishmen, and the thoughts of the victories they were to win induced the natives to labour on.

Dick had followed his own plan of notching the days on sticks, several of which he had tied up in a bundle. By his calculation we had been two years among the savages, and I could now speak their language perfectly well. Our clothes were worn out, and I had to dress like the natives. The chief told me, when I grew older, that I must be tattooed, an operation for which I had no fancy, and I hoped to make my escape before he should insist on my undergoing it.

The vessel was at last built, and ready to be launched. She was a schooner of about forty tons, and capable of carrying sixty or eighty men. The natives declared that none of their island canoes would be able to contend with her. It took some time to rig her, and to obtain suitable provisions and casks for holding water.

I don't know whether Motakee suspected the design of the Englishmen; but when I spoke of taking a cruise in her, he replied that he would not expose me to the dangers she might encounter, and I found that I was more narrowly watched than ever.

Dick came back one day, looking very much out of spirits.

"The other men have formed a plan for escaping, but I

cannot agree to it," he said. "They intend to let as many natives as choose to come on board, and, as soon as they are out of sight of land, to rise upon them and heave them overboard, so that their provisions and water should not be exhausted, should they have to make a long voyage. And another thing is, Charley, I won't go without you."

Motakee had not entered into the views of his countrymen with regard to the vessel the Englishmen were building: he either suspected their design or believed that she would not prove as successful in attacking their foes as the rest supposed. When I asked his leave to go on board, he took me by the arm and whispered—

"I know your tricks; you should not have told me how you managed to get away and join your friend. No, no; I shall shut you up till the vessel has sailed."

He was as good as his word, and from that day I was not allowed to leave the hut without the company of one of his most trusted followers. He allowed Dick, however, to go about as he chose, apparently caring but little whether or not he made his escape.

Dick had been absent for three days. I could not believe that he had gone without me, and yet I felt very anxious about him. On the fourth day he returned.

"They have gone, Charley," he exclaimed; "all our people and thirty natives. I stopped to the last, trying to persuade them to give up their wicked plan; but they answered that the natives had murdered our friends and burned our ship, and that they had a right to treat them as they chose. I said that I was sure we ought not to return evil for evil, and that they might have found some other way of making their escape, and that no good could possibly come of what they were about. They abused me, and asked me if I was going to betray them, and that if I would not come with them, I must take the consequences, as the natives were sure to murder us, as soon as they discovered what had become of their countrymen. Even now I think I was wrong in not warning Motakee, for I consented to evil, though I would not join in it."

When Motakee found that the schooner had sailed, he allowed me to go about as usual, and treated Dick with far more respect than before. Dick, indeed, soon became his right-hand man, or councillor, and the people looked up to him as the person next to the chief, in consequence.

Some days after this it came on to blow very hard, and the sea beat with tremendous fury on the rocky coast. Dick and I wished to have a sight of the huge breakers outside the harbour. We went along the shore for some distance, to a part exposed to the whole sweep of the ocean. As we were looking along it, Dick exclaimed that he saw a vessel on the rocks. We made our way as near as we could get to the spot.

"Charley, I am afraid that is the schooner," Dick exclaimed; "but there is not a living being on board."

We crept on still closer to the little vessel. We shouted loudly, lest any one might have been washed on shore, but no reply came to our cries.

"I am afraid every one has been washed away," he observed. "If the natives had been on board, they are such first-rate swimmers that some of them would have managed to reach the land."

We looked about in every direction, but could discover no boats on the beach nor any sign of a living man.

"It's too likely that our people did as they intended, and having got rid of the natives, were themselves caught in the hurricane and driven back here; but we shall never know, I suspect, what has happened."

After spending a considerable time in searching about, being unable to get nearer the wreck, we returned home. We told Motakee what we had seen; but, of course, did not mention our suspicions.

"I knew that the voyage would work us no good, to your people or mine," he observed; "and I am very glad you did not sail in the vessel."

We were, indeed, thankful that we had not.

Next day, when the hurricane was over, we went back with some of the natives to examine the wreck; but, on getting on board, we could find nothing to explain the mystery. Dick's opinion was that the crew had been on deck, and were washed overboard before the vessel struck, some time after they had disposed of the unfortunate natives in the way they had proposed.

I have not spoken of the various events which had taken place since we came to the island. Several times Motakee had gone out to fight his enemies, and had invariably returned victorious.

At length another expedition was talked of against a powerful tribe at some distance. He told Dick he must prepare to accompany him. I begged that I might go, too.

"No, Charley; you must stay at home," answered Dick. "I have no wish to go and fight other savages in a quarrel in which I have no concern, and I would not go if I could stay away without offending the chief. I don't want to kill any of the fellows, and I don't wish to be killed either."

The warriors were preparing to take their departure, when, early in the morning, as I was looking out over the sea, I caught sight of a ship approaching the island. I watched her eagerly, and when, at length, I felt sure she was standing towards the harbour, I ran back to tell Dick. The natives had been so busy in preparing their weapons, that they had not observed her. Fortunately, no one saw me.

"Now is our chance, then," exclaimed Dick. "Come along, Charley: we will jump into a canoe, and maybe we shall get away from the shore before the savages miss us."

Without a moment's delay we hurried down to the beach, taking some paddles out of a canoe-hut on our way. We launched a canoe, which we found hauled up on the shore, and paddled with might and main out to sea. The water was smooth, and, though the wind was against us, we made good progress. The ship came on. We were alongside. Ropes were hove-to us, and, making the canoe fast, we scrambled up on deck.

CHAPTER SEVENTEEN

ESCAPE FROM THE ISLAND

"Some savages come on board, sir," I heard the mate sing out to the captain, a fine-looking man, who was standing near the wheel; "an old and a young one."

"No, please you, sir," said Dick, stepping aft. "We are not savages, but unfortunate Englishmen. We have had a hard job to make our escape from the savages, though, and if you will take my advice, sir, you will not go into that harbour; for if you do, you will run a chance of being treated as our ship was."

"How is that, my man?" asked the captain; and Dick thereupon told him the way in which the *Dolphin* had been cut off, and how all had been kept prisoners for upwards of two years by the natives.

"I thank you for the warning, my friend," said the captain, "and we will be on our guard against treachery. I think, however, that if we show that we are well armed and on the watch, we need not fear them. We are in want of water, wood, and vegetables, and by letting the natives understand that we will pay fairly for them, we shall, I hope, obtain what we require."

W. H. G. Kingston

"As to that, sir, Charley Laurel and I can talk well enough to them; and we will take good care to tell them that they must play no tricks."

"You may be of much service to me, then," said the captain, "and I shall be glad to carry you and Charley Laurel, as you call him, to any place we touch at where you may wish to land."

"Thank you, sir," said Dick; "but we can both work our passage, and though it is better than two years since I was afloat, I don't think I am less handy than before."

The ship, which we found to be the *Phoebe*, Captain Renton, having brought up in the bay, a number of canoes came off to her. The captain told me and Dick to say to them that he could allow no one on board. The natives looked much surprised at seeing us on the deck, and they of course guessing that we had told the captain what had happened to the *Dolphin*, some of them paddled back again in a great fright, supposing that he had come to punish them for what they had done. By the captain's directions we told them not to be alarmed; that he wished to be friends with them; and that if they behaved well, they would be treated as friends.

In a short time Motakee came off. When we told Captain Renton who he was, he was invited on deck. He seemed greatly concerned at the thought of losing me, and asked me reproachfully how, after being treated as a son, I could think of deserting him. I assured him that I was very grateful for all his kindness, but that I wished to go back to live among people of my own colour and habits, and that otherwise I would gladly have remained with him. He soon made himself at home on board, and when invited into the cabin behaved with great propriety, and told me to express to the captain his regret for the massacre of the *Dolphin's* crew.

He put off his expedition on account of the arrival of the *Phoebe*, and while she remained in harbour he was constantly on board, and used every exertion to obtain what the captain wanted.

I at last parted from him with real regret, though Dick would not let me venture on shore, lest he might show his affection for me by keeping me a prisoner.

Captain Renton was a very different sort of person to poor Captain Podgers. We had prayers every evening in his cabin, and he would allow none of the officers to use abusive language towards the men, while he maintained strict discipline on board.

He proposed cruising for some time for whales in those latitudes, and then sailing south, to touch at one of the Society Islands.

The day after we sailed, the captain called me into his cabin.

"I have heard your history, my lad, from your friend, Dick Driver, and I find that you have had no advantages of education, while I am afraid that you are very ignorant of gospel truth, without which all education is of no avail in God's sight."

"As I have not seen a book since I was on board the *Dolphin*, I suspect that I should prove a bad hand at reading, sir," I answered: "but I have not forgotten what Miss Kitty told me about the love of Jesus to sinful man; how He willingly offered Himself up to be punished instead of us, that all who believe on Him may be free, and be able to go to God as children go to an affectionate father, and ask Him for all they want; and that when we die we may be sure that we shall be taken to live with Him in great joy and happiness for ever and ever."

"Ah, my dear boy," exclaimed the captain, his eye brightening with pleasure, "you already know then the most important truths I can tell you. And do you indeed believe that Jesus died for you, and is your Saviour, and loves you, and watches over you, and sends His Holy Spirit to help you to love Him, and serve Him, and to keep you out of temptation?"

"Yes, indeed I do, sir," I answered. "I pray to God through Him every night and morning, and I believe that He has preserved me from the many dangers I have gone through."

Though I have not mentioned it, I had often talked with Dick of all Miss Kitty had taught me, and the knowledge of God's love more than anything else had supported us; and I am very sure that Dick felt as I did, though he might not have been able to explain himself so clearly. I had made great progress indeed under Miss Kitty's instruction; thus, although for some time I at first found it difficult to read the New Testament, which the captain put into my hands, I gradually regained the knowledge I had lost.

The kind captain, after the conversation I have mentioned, invited me into the cabin every day, and took great pains in instructing me in reading and writing. Until I could do so myself, he read a portion of God's Word, which he explained to me in a very simple and clear manner. I did my utmost to learn, as I was now of an age to be ashamed of my ignorance, especially when I found that the two ship's boys read and wrote far better than I did. Every moment that I was off duty I was at my studies, and when Dick found what progress I made, he declared his intention of setting to work to learn to read himself. I did my best to help him, and the captain kindly lent him some books that he might instruct himself. In about four months I could read with perfect ease and write very fairly, besides having gained some knowledge of arithmetic and geography. As to history, I found I had a very confused knowledge, and jumbled events together in a curious way.

I had not forgotten dear Miss Kitty, and I often talked about her, and wondered whether she and the mate had made their escape. Dick always said that he thought they had, as Mr Falconer was a good navigator, and that they were very likely to have fallen in with some whaler, as he was sure to have steered his course over the ground most frequented by them.

At length, after sailing for some time south, and passing several islands, we sighted one at which the captain said he intended to touch, as the natives were Christians, and they could supply all his wants on equitable terms, without the risk of treachery, which he must run at the heathen islands. As we drew near I recognised the scenery, and on asking Dick, he told me it was the very island at which the *Dolphin* had touched when Miss Kitty and Mr Falconer had gone on shore to the house of the missionary.

As soon as the anchor was down, the captain ordered a boat to be lowered, and told me that I might accompany him.

Mr Newton, the missionary, who knew Captain Renton, came down to the landing-place to welcome him, and conduct him up to his house. I followed, but as he did not recognise me, I felt unwilling to address him. They entered the house together.

"Come in, my lad," said Mr Newton, seeing me standing outside. "You are heartily welcome."

I followed the captain into the sitting-room, where I saw two

W. H. G. Kingston

ladies. One, whom I guessed was Mrs Newton, came forward to greet him as an old acquaintance; the other rose, and as she did so and turned her face towards me, my heart leaped with joy, for there I saw Miss Kitty, looking as bright and blooming as ever.

"Miss Kitty!" I exclaimed; "is it you? is it you?"

The first moment she did not know me, for I was greatly changed. She took both my hands, and looking into my face, she said—

"Charley, Charley Laurel, are you indeed alive and well? I had greatly feared that you were lost. And has honest Dick too escaped?"

She made me sit down by her side, and I rapidly told her all that had occurred.

"And how did you escape, Miss Kitty?" I asked; "we were fearfully anxious about you."

"You had reason to be so," she answered. "Mr Falconer had expressed some fears that the natives might prove treacherous while we were away in the boats, and, on our return, he was remarking that he must try and induce the captain to keep a strict watch on board, and to allow only a few natives at a time on deck, when, through his glass, he observed that the ship was surrounded by canoes, and that the natives in great numbers were clambering on board. Still we sailed on, when we saw a dreadful explosion, and shortly afterwards several canoes came paddling after us. Mr Falconer pointed them out to the men, who agreed with him that the ship had been taken by the savages, and that by some accident they had blown her up. He immediately put the boat about, exclaiming to me, 'For your sake we will do our best to escape!' The wind increased: we were standing out into the open ocean. Had it not been on my account Mr Falconer would, I am sure, have gone back at all risks to ascertain the fate of those on board. The fact, however, of the canoes following us, showed the hostile intentions of the natives, and the men declared that even had I not been in the boat they would not have run their heads into danger for no purpose.

"As the wind increased we lost sight of the canoes, which were unable to contend with the heavy sea to which the boat was now exposed.

"The prospect before us was a fearful one, but the alternative of returning to the shore was worse. Still we could rely on the protecting care of our heavenly Father, in whom we both trusted. We had but a small supply of food and water, which, with the greatest economy, could only last us three days. Mr Falconer, however, encouraged the men by telling them that he hoped, before the end of that time, to make an island, marked as uninhabited on the chart, where we might obtain water and provisions.

"Happily the wind, though continuing fair, did not increase, and, exactly at the time Mr Falconer expected, the island appeared in sight, when the last drop of water had been exhausted. Coasting around the island, we found a small harbour, which we entered. A grove of cocoa-nut trees greeted our sight, fringing the shore, and near them was a spring of fresh water. Mr Falconer shot several birds, and having fishing-hooks and lines, the men quickly caught a supply of fish. They then put up a hut for me, where I could enjoy that rest I so much required. At night, also, a number of turtle were observed landing on the sandy beach to lay their eggs, and we thus had no longer any fear of suffering from starvation.

"So well satisfied were the men with the island, that they proposed remaining, rather than venture again to sea. Mr Falconer inquired my wishes. I knew that I could implicitly trust him. Months would perhaps pass before any ship might appear. I begged that, if the men would be persuaded to go, we might continue our voyage. They agreed at length to do as he wished.

"Besides the casks, a number of cocoa-nuts were filled with water; birds, and fish, and turtle, were salted, and four live turtle and a number of cocoa-nuts were taken on board. Thus amply supplied with provisions, we again set sail.

"We had been a week at sea, when a vessel was seen, hove-to in the distance. We steered for her. Her boats were away in chase of a whale. We received a kind welcome on board the ship, which was the *Harmony*, from Captain Landon and his wife, who were Christian people. My satisfaction was very great when I found that the captain intended touching at this island, to refit his ship before proceeding to other fishing-grounds. The second mate had died, and he offered Mr Falconer the berth. He gladly accepted it. At the end of three weeks I had the happiness of finding myself with these kind friends.

"I knew how Mr Falconer felt when he told me that he must continue on board the *Harmony*, though he trusted on his arrival in England to be able to obtain the command of a ship in which he might return here. Since then no letter from him has reached me, nor have I received any tidings of him. Still I feel perfect confidence that he is faithful and true, and that he will return as soon as he can find the means of doing so."

I felt very sorry when I heard the latter part of Miss Kitty's narrative; for while I fully agreed with her that Mr Falconer would return if he could, I feared that, had he not lost his life, he might have been wrecked or taken prisoner, or detained somewhere by illness.

As Mr Newton afterwards observed to me, he had never seen any woman who was so thoroughly sustained under a great trial by her confidence in the man to whom she had given her heart, and her perfect trust that all was ordered by God for the best.

CHAPTER EIGHTEEN

ON STILTS

I felt very sorry at the thought of leaving Miss Kitty, and would gladly have remained with her and Mr and Mrs Newton, but Dick would not hear of my doing so; and Captain Renton insisted that I should return home with him, and go to school and obtain that instruction which I certainly greatly required.

"We will take good care of the young lady, Charley," said Mr Newton; "and should you meet with Mr Falconer, tell him that she is still as well cared for as at first."

Once more the *Phoebe* was at sea. Captain Renton gave me a berth in his cabin, and took so much pains to instruct me, that before the voyage was over I had made good progress in various branches of knowledge.

"Why, Charley," said Dick, who was proud of the information I displayed, "you have become quite a scholar. Should not be surprised to hear of your bearing up to be a judge, or a bishop, or a big-wig of some sort."

"No, no, Dick," I answered; "my only wish is to be a sailor, though I own I should like to be a captain some day or other, though, of course, I must study to become that."

"No fear of you, if you go on as you have begun," remarked Dick, gazing approvingly at me.

We were about the latitude of Madeira, when one morning we sighted a ship standing to the south'ard. As the day drew on, just as we were close to her, it fell calm, and she made a signal that she would send letters on board us to carry home. A boat put off from her, and came alongside. The second mate of the ship came on deck with the letters.

"Captain Falconer, of the *Harmony*, begs that you will post these on your arrival in England," he said, presenting them to Captain Renton, by whose side I was standing.

"Captain Falconer!" I exclaimed, turning eagerly to my captain. "May I go on board and see him, sir? I cannot help thinking that he was the mate of the *Dolphin*, who saved that young lady from the savages."

Captain Renton at once ordered a boat to be lowered, to carry me on board the *Harmony*, letting Dick accompany me. Dick, who pulled the stroke-oar, gave way with a will, for he felt as eager as I was about the matter. We were soon alongside, and without waiting for the mate, who commanded the boat, I scrambled on board, followed by Dick. There, to my great delight, I saw Mr Falconer. He did not recognise me, as without ceremony I hurried aft, but when he saw Dick, he started, and then looked inquiringly at me.

"What, are you Dick Driver?" he exclaimed, as Dick, not forgetting his manners, touched his hat to him.

"Yes, sir. I am myself, and I am right glad to see you alive and well; and this is Charley Laurel, who, may be, you remember."

"Indeed I do," said Mr Falconer, shaking me warmly by the hand, and inviting us down in his cabin. "I feared that you had been both killed by the savages."

I briefly narrated how we had escaped, and when I told him that we had visited Mr Newton, and left Miss Kitty well, only a few months before, I judged by the agitation and interest he showed that she had not misplaced her confidence in him.

"I am bound out to the South Seas, where I have hitherto in vain attempted to go," he observed. "As soon as I reached England, I obtained a berth on board a ship bound for the Pacific, but she was unhappily wrecked not far from Cape Horn. I, with some of the crew who had reached the land, was taken off by a homeward-bound ship, in which I returned to England. I should immediately have again sailed, but hearing that my father was ill, I went to visit him. I had the happiness of being reconciled to him before he died, when I found myself the possessor of a small fortune. It is not, however, sufficient to enable me to live without a profession, and through the recommendation of the late captain of the *Harmony*, which her owners were about to send again to the Pacific, I obtained command of her, and trust before long of again having the happiness of seeing Miss Raglan."

"I am sure, sir, she will be very glad to see you," I could not help saying; and I told him that none of his letters had been received.

Captain Falconer kept me on board all day, and nearly the whole time was spent by him in asking me questions, and hearing all I could tell him about Miss Kitty. In the evening, he sent me and Dick back to the *Phoebe* in one of the *Harmony's* boats.

Next morning a westerly breeze sprang up, and the two ships stood on their respective courses.

After this we had a quick run to England, and, arriving in the Thames, Captain Renton took me with him to the owners, Messrs. Dear and Ashe, to whom he gave an account of my adventures. Mr Dear, the head of the firm, was a mild-looking pleasant old gentleman. He called me into his room, and asked me a number of questions, and then desired Captain Renton to send Dick Driver next day up to the office.

"If you can spare the lad, I will take him home with me, as Mrs Dear will like to see him," he observed.

"I intended to have taken you to my house, Charley," said Captain Renton, as he wished me good-bye, "but I am sure it will be to your advantage to accept Mr Dear's invitation."

In the afternoon, I drove out with Mr Dear to his country house, in the neighbourhood of London. It appeared to me a perfect palace. I had never before since I could recollect been in any house larger than Mr Newton's cottage.

Mrs Dear, a very kind lady, soon made me feel perfectly at home.

"We are much interested in you, Charley," she said, "and Mr Dear will do his best to discover your relations in the West Indies. In the mean time we think you will benefit by going to school."

I was very sorry to leave Captain Renton, but said I was

ready to do whatever she and Mr Dear thought best.

The next evening, when Mr Dear returned, he said that he could not ascertain from Dick Driver the name of the island from which I had been taken away. At the same time he observed: "I conclude that I shall be able to learn at the Admiralty what place it was the *Laurel* and her consorts attacked."

I spent a couple of weeks with my new friends before they found a school to which I could be sent. Captain Renton, accompanied by Dick, came out to see me. Dick had agreed to sail again in the *Phoebe*, and promised that, on his return, he would not fail to pay me a visit. He looked very downcast.

"We have been together for the best part of ten years, Charley," he said, as he wrung my hand, "and if I did not know it was for your good, I could not bear the thoughts of parting from you; but you are in kind hands, and I know it's better for you to remain on shore, and I am not one to stand in your way—I love you too well for that."

The next day Mr Dear drove me down to a large school at Hammersmith. I was introduced to the master, Mr Rushton, a tall gentleman with white hair, who looked very well able to keep a number of boys in order, and Mr Dear gave him a brief account of my history.

"The lad will do very well," he said, patting me on the head. "I have boys from all parts of the world, and he will soon find himself at home among them."

As soon as Mr Dear had gone, Mr Rushton, taking me by the hand, led me into the playground, where upwards of a hundred boys were rushing about, engaged in all sorts of games. He shouted "Fenwick," and a boy of my own age came up. He told the boy that he wished him to look after me, and teach me the ways of the school. Having done this, he re-entered the house.

As soon as the master was gone, I found myself surrounded by a number of boys, who, having examined me from head to foot, began asking me questions.

Though I was ignorant of all their games, and had scarcely heard of cricket and football, yet I knew a number of things which they did not.

"Who is your father?" asked one fellow.

"I don't know," I replied.

"Who is your mother?" inquired another.

I gave the same answer, whereon there was a general laugh.

"Have you many brothers and sisters?"

"I don't know," I again said.

"Where were you born?"

"That's more than I can tell you," I answered, quite quietly, and so I went on.

"I don't think you have got much out of me," I said, at last. "And now I want to know who among you can box the compass? Can any of you put a ship about? Can some one describe the Marquesas? or tell me where Tahiti and the Sandwich Islands are to be found?"

To none of these or similar questions did I receive any replies.

"Now I find that I have not got much out of you, either," I observed, "so we are pretty equal. Now, you might have answered my questions, though no one, as far as I know, could have answered those you put to me."

"The young fellow has got his wits about him," observed one of the big boys; and the others at once seemed inclined to treat me with far more respect than at first.

"Now," said I, gaining courage, "I have spent most of my life at sea, where we don't play the games you have on shore, but if any of you will teach me, I shall be very glad to learn them; and perhaps I may show you how to do a number of things you know nothing about."

From that day forward I was never bothered by having questions put to me. I soon managed to get hold of a piece of rope, which had lashed up one of the boy's boxes, and began to initiate several who wished to learn into the mysteries of knotting and splicing. Before long a carpenter came to do some work, and I got him to make me a pair of stilts. Several of the bigger boys ordered others. I would not use mine till the rest came home. Many then tried to walk about on them.

"Who are going to try their stilts?" I asked.

"We want to see you, Laurel, walk on yours," was the answer.

"No, no; you mount on yours first," I said; and most of them tried to get up, each with the help of two or three fellows who stood round to support them. I then brought out mine.

"Shall we help you?" inquired three or four of the boys, who by this time were my chief friends and supporters.

"Thank you," I said, laughing; while the others who were looking on expected to see me bungle as the rest had been doing. My friends collected round me and prepared to help me up. I did not undeceive them, but suddenly jumping on one side I sprang into my stilts.

"Who's for a race?" I cried out. "Come along; let us start fair."

We were at one end of the playground, and I began to move backwards and forwards, and in and out among the other fellows. They seemed satisfied that I was not going to do much better than they were. Several who had by this time managed to balance themselves, now formed a line.

"Away you go," cried one of the big boys, who expected to see me and the rest tumble down on our noses.

Off we started. In an instant I felt as much at home as I had been when making my escape from Motakee's village, and, as might be supposed, away I went. First one of the boys tumbled down, then another, and another, while I kept ahead, and, reaching the end of the playground, turned back again, to find all my competitors rubbing their arms and knees, only two or three having the courage to make an attempt to stand up again on their stilts.

"I don't want to laugh at you," I said, as I came back and stalked in and out among them, looking down with a complacent air from my lofty elevation. "I ought to have told you, perhaps, that I have had some experience in walking on stilts, though, as I had not used them for many months, I did not wish to boast beforehand. You will do as well as I can in time."

"I should think you must have had experience," cried out two or three of the big fellows; "and probably you can do a good many more things. We shall be on the watch not to be taken in again."

Stilt-walking soon became the rage, though I continued to be far superior to all my companions. They looked up to me in consequence with even greater respect than before, and I found my position in the school as satisfactory as I could desire. I was able, consequently, to take the part of many of the weaker or less courageous boys who were bullied by the rest. Among others, there was a delicate boy called Henri de Villereine, and who, because he spoke with a foreign accent, was nicknamed Frenchy. Though a year or two my senior, he was not nearly so strong, and was ill able to defend himself against much smaller boys. He seemed a gentle, well-disposed boy, and when others, on my first going to school, had attacked me, he had always stood aloof. Though I had not had much conversation with him, I could not bear to see him bullied.

One day, when two or three fellows had set upon him, I rushed up to his assistance, and, without saying a word, knocked over his assailants one after the other. He gratefully thanked me, and said he was afraid that, as soon as my back was turned, the fellows would set on him again.

After this no one ventured to attack Henri de Villereine, and I was the means of rendering his life at school far pleasanter, poor fellow! than it had been before. He showed his gratitude by every means in his power, and as I liked him for his many amiable qualities, we became fast friends.

However, I have not space to give an account of my

schoolboy days. I applied myself diligently to my studies, and while I believe that I was liked by the boys, I gained credit with the masters, and rose rapidly towards the head of the school.

W. H. G. Kingston

CHAPTER NINETEEN

DICK'S LESSON NOT LOST

I had been three years at school, and was now almost a man in appearance. Henri had gone to the island of Saint Lucia in the West Indies, where his family resided. I was sorry to lose him, as there was no boy in the school I liked so much. He had made me promise to come and see him should I ever be able to do so. This seemed not impossible, as I had not lost my affection for the sea, and Mr Dear had promised to send me in one of his ships, should I wish to follow it as a profession. I had, indeed, thought of no other.

He had made all the inquiries he could to discover my friends, but hitherto unsuccessfully.

I had spent my holidays at his house, when he and his wife treated me as kindly as if I had been their son.

The midsummer holidays were approaching. We had a large cricket-field just opposite the house, where one evening we were playing. I had become as good a cricketer as any of the big boys, though I never cared very much for that or any other game which seemed to lead to no result. I liked it, as it gave exercise to the body, just as I like chess because it requires mental exertion. My side was in, and I had just given up my bat, having been caught out, when, as I was going to throw myself down on the grass, I saw a sailor-like looking man enter the field. He looked about for some time. I went towards him and inquired what he wanted.

"Can you tell me, sir, if young Charley Laurel is at this school, and whereabouts I can find him?" he said, addressing me as a stranger.

The moment he spoke my heart leaped into my mouth, for I recognised my faithful friend and protector, Dick Driver. I could scarcely resist throwing my arms round his neck, as I should have done when a little boy, but the fancy seized me to try whether he would find out who I was when I spoke.

"Charley Laurel, the young monkey. You don't suppose a big fellow like me would take the trouble to be looking after such a little jackanapes; but if you care for him, I shall be happy to try and find him out for you."

"Care for him? I should think I do: he has never been out of my head all these years I have been away from home. I brought him up, I may say, since he was no higher than my knee, and I love him as if he had been my own son."

I had led Dick, as he was speaking, to a shady spot under some tall trees on one side of the field, away from the rest of the fellows.

"I am sure you do, Dick; and Charley would be an ungrateful fellow if he did not love you from the bottom of his heart," I answered.

Dick looked hard at me as I spoke, then grasping my hands, which I held out, he exclaimed:

W. H. G. Kingston

"Why, as I live, you are Charley yourself! My dear, dear boy, what has come over my eyes, that I should not have known you? and yet, to be sure you are grown into a fine big fellow."

I assured Dick that I had known him at once, and begged his pardon for the trick I had played him.

We sat down on the grass, and, as may be supposed, had a long yarn together.

Dick, as I knew, had sailed again in the *Phoebe* another voyage to the Pacific, and had only just returned.

"To my mind, Charley, it's high time that you should go to sea, if you are going at all, or you will never get rid of your land ways—not that I have any fear of you now. The *Phoebe* is going into dock to receive a thorough repair, and I have promised Captain Renton to rejoin him as soon as she is ready for sea; and I feel sure, if you apply to the owners, they will appoint you. I set my heart on having you with me, and, to tell you the truth, I should not be happy without you. So just you ask them, and they will not say 'nay.'"

I told Dick there was nothing I so much wished, and promised at once to write and ask Mr Dear. Dick was greatly pleased.

"The matter is settled then, Charley, and I hope, before many months are over, we shall be in blue water together again, and I shall be teaching you many of the things which I am afraid all your schooling must have made you forget." As it was a half-holiday, I was able to spend several hours with Dick. We were at length discovered. The boys gathered round us, inquiring who Dick was; and on hearing that he was an old sailor, begged him to spin them some of his yarns. Dick indulged them to their hearts' content, and, among other things, narrated some of the early events of my life. At last he was obliged to take his departure, that he might catch the evening coach for London.

When the school broke up, I returned to Mr Dear's. He at once questioned me as to my inclinations about a profession; and when I told him that I wished to go to sea, he replied, to my great joy, that he would make arrangements for my sailing in the *Phoebe*.

I spent several weeks at his house, before she was ready for sea, employing my time, at his suggestion, in studying navigation.

On going up to town one day, I found Captain Renton at the office. He cordially welcomed me, and assured Mr Dear that he would do his best to make a sailor of me, and to fit me for my duties as an officer.

The *Phoebe* was, I found, bound out to Sydney, New South Wales. As she was by this time nearly ready for sea, Mr Dear thought it best that I should go on board at once and commence my duties. I found that Dick had already joined.

"I hope, Charley, you have not forgotten what you knew before you went to school," he observed. "I have been mortally afraid that the book-learning would drive your seamanship out of your head."

"I hope not," I answered; "I feel myself perfectly at home already, but I shall be able to judge better when I get to sea."

When Captain Renton left the ship that evening, I thought he looked very pale; and the next day the first mate, Mr Gibbs, received a message to say that he was too ill to come on board. Several days passed. We then heard that he was unable to proceed on the voyage, and had given up the command to a Captain Slack, who made his appearance the next morning.

"I don't like his name," observed Dick to me, "but he may be a very good man for all that: still, to my eye, he is very different to Captain Renton, but we shall find out all about him by-and-by."

At length the *Phoebe* went out of dock down to Gravesend. Some of her passengers had already come on board, the rest here joined us.

We soon found when we got into blue water that Captain Slack was, as Dick feared, a very different sort of person from Captain Renton. We had no services on a Sunday, no prayers in the cabin; and, though he had appeared quiet enough in harbour, he now swore at the men and abused the officers if anything went wrong. Had Mr Dear known the sort of man he was, I feel sure that he would not have given him the command of the ship. The passengers seemed very indifferent to his conduct, as long as he did not abuse them, and that he took very good care not to do.

"Charley, I hope you have not forgotten to say your prayers," said Dick to me, one day. "The more ungodly people are around us, the more need there seems to me that we should pray to be led aright, and kept from joining in their wickedness. You have got your Bible with you, I hope."

I had, but I had to confess that I had not once looked into it.

"I have not sailed so many years with good Captain Renton, without learning his ways, and as I want to be guided by the Bible, I am very sure that I must read it every day.

Sometimes I find it a difficult job, but I don't mind the other men laughing and jeering at me, as they are fond of doing; neither, Charley, will you, if you are wise. It is better to fear God, than poor helpless beings like ourselves. That's what I always say to myself when the others begin to jeer at me."

I promised Dick that I would do as he advised, and that very day when I went to my berth, on the half-deck, I got out my Bible and began to read it. I remembered what Captain Renton often said to me, that I must not read it like a common book, but that I must earnestly pray to be enlightened by God's Holy Spirit while I read it, to understand its truths. I did so, and I then saw that I was an utterly lost sinner, and, as far as my own merits were concerned, had no right to claim admittance into heaven. But then I saw also, that by trusting to the merits of Christ, and to His perfect and complete sacrifice offered up for me, my sins were washed away, and that God would receive me and welcome me as a dear son; and that at any moment, should I be called out of the world, I should be sure of eternal happiness. I also learned another glorious truth, namely, that Christ the great High Priest, who has entered into the Holy of Holies, is now at the right hand of God, and having taken my flesh upon Him, knows all my infirmities, and can be touched by them, having been tempted as I am, and thus acts as my mediator, my intercessor, my advocate; thus washing me daily, hourly, every moment, with His blood, from the sins which I commit. Yet I know that every sin grieves and offends Him, and I strive with the aid of His Holy Spirit to resist sin, to refrain from sin, and I sorrow heartily for the sins of which I know I am guilty. Yet I live in a constant sense of His boundless love and mercy. I do so now, I did so then. This gave me a contentment and joy I had never known before, and I no longer feared any danger, nor felt cast down by the annoyances which my ungodly shipmates were continually endeavouring to give me.

W. H. G. Kingston

This knowledge, however, did not come all at once, and many weeks passed by before I attained to that happy condition which I am sure all Christians ought to enjoy. I at length spoke to Dick on the subject.

"Of course, Charley," he said, "it's a poor religion to my mind if a man does not take God at His word and believe what He says; and He tells us that all who believe on His Son have passed from death unto life, have entered the kingdom of heaven, and are heirs of eternal happiness. It seems to me all clear sailing when we know that, though Satan is always trying to place rocks and quicksands in our way, but when we have got the true Pilot aboard, we are sure to keep clear of them, for He can make no mistake. That makes me happy and contented, and afraid of nothing except that I should forget to pray for that help, which, if I pray, is sure to be sent me."

Dick and I, knowing that we were not to keep our light under a bushel, as we had the opportunities, spoke to others, and by degrees several of the crew joined us to read the Bible and pray together.

The captain heard of our proceedings, and, declaring that he would have no prayers or psalm-singers on board, Dick was summoned aft to answer for his conduct.

"I only do what Captain Renton did, sir," he answered, quietly; "and if I neglect my duty, I do not ask to be treated with more favour than others."

"Just take care what you are about then," answered the captain; "my eye will be upon you."

Dick touched his hat respectfully, and without saying anything went forward.

I was soon afterwards called up.

"I should have expected, Mr Laurel, that you would have known better than to try and upset the discipline of the ship," he observed, in a sarcastic tone. "How can you expect the men to obey me if you try and make them suppose that they are better than I am?"

"I am not attempting to do so, Captain Slack," I answered, quietly. "The more I read the Bible, the more clearly I see that it is the duty of Christians to obey those set in authority over them; and I am very sure that those of the crew who follow its precepts will become more obedient seamen and more anxious to do their duty than heretofore."

"As to that, I am a better judge than a youngster who has only just left school," he observed; "and I warn you, as I warned your friend, to take care of what you are about."

As we were only doing what his predecessor had encouraged, the captain did not dare to prohibit our meetings, and Dick and I continued as before to read our Bibles, and to induce all we could to listen. The third mate and one of the midshipmen, as well as several of the seamen and passengers, joined us, though the rest seemed more than ever determined to reject the truth, and to go on in their old ways.

As we neared Sydney, the captain resumed his shore-going manners, and did his best to make himself agreeable to the passengers.

On a fine morning, soon after daybreak, we entered the magnificent harbour of Port Jackson. As soon as the passengers had landed and the cargo was discharged, we had to turn to and prepare the ship for sea, so I had little opportunity of visiting the place. As we had orders to clean up the cabins, we knew that we were to take passengers home; and having received a cargo of wool, "Blue Peter" was hoisted, as a sign that we were ready to sail. Several passengers immediately came on board: among the last was a gentleman, who, by his dress, I knew to be a missionary or clergyman, and two ladies who accompanied him. No sooner had the younger lady stepped on deck than I felt sure she was my old friend Miss Kitty. I ran eagerly up to her. Her surprise was even greater than mine, for she did not recollect me. Her companions were Mr and Mrs Newton. They all expressed their pleasure at seeing me, and told me that they had come to Sydney, on their way to England.

Miss Kitty looked very sad. I was afraid of asking about Captain Falconer, fearing that something painful might have occurred connected with him. I waited, hoping to hear his name mentioned. At length I made the inquiry of Mr Newton.

"He has paid us two visits, and is still in these seas, though hoping soon to return home," he answered. "He is as much attached as ever to our friend, but he is wisely anxious to secure the comforts of a home before he marries; and though she would not have refused to become his wife, had he pressed her, still, believing that her father is alive, and may return home, she wishes first to obtain his sanction."

With a favourable breeze, the *Phoebe* soon ran the coast of Australia out of sight.

CHAPTER TWENTY

OVERBOARD

We had been some weeks at sea. Captain Slack showed his evil disposition by throwing every impediment in the way of Mr Newton when he attempted to hold a service on board. He could not, however, prevent him from having prayers in his own cabin, to which I and Dick, and those who were willing to come, were invited. Among them was a half-caste lad, called Bill Gennill, of a not over-prepossessing countenance, to whom I had spoken. While others scoffed, he listened, and had before we reached Sydney gladly accepted the truth. This exposed him to the sneers, and often to the ill-treatment, of his messmates, though Dick and I did our best to protect him. He expressed his gratitude, and, opposing gentleness to brutality, showed every day more and more earnestness. Mr Newton encouraged him to persevere. Miss Kitty often spoke kindly to him, and frequently brought up her Bible, and read such portions as he could best understand.

"I think that Bill understands the fundamental truths of the gospel," she said to me: "that being all sinners by nature, and outcasts from God, and become again His dear children by simple faith in the glorious fact that Christ died, and was punished instead of us, and that our debt to God being thus

W. H. G. Kingston

paid, our sins are blotted out of His remembrance, and that we being clothed with the righteousness of Christ, we can approach boldly the throne of grace, and are made heirs with Him of that kingdom which He has gone before to prepare for us. He knows, too, that, being possessed of these privileges, we are called on by the aid of the Holy Spirit to try and imitate Christ, to live pure and blameless lives, to make His name known to others, and do all the good we can to our fellow-creatures, especially to those of the household of faith. I am thankful to find, Charley, that you, too, know these truths, and are not ashamed of Christ."

"I have not understood them many months, though I ought to have known them long ago," I answered. "Now that I do know them, I feel that nothing is so disgraceful to a Christian as to be ashamed of confessing the Master he serves, and therefore it is that Satan is always endeavouring to make us conceal our belief in the presence of our fellow-men. I feel how necessary it is to pray for grace for those who do not really acknowledge Christ, although they would be very angry if told that they were not Christians."

"I found that to be the case in Sydney," said Miss Kitty, "although during the time I spent with Mr and Mrs Newton it was a difficulty I did not experience. The poor heathens among whom I lived were sincere; they had discovered the worthlessness of their own idols, and felt their sinfulness, and, consequently, heard with joy the simple plan of salvation which God in His mercy has prepared for man. In Sydney, I found people so well satisfied with their forms and ceremonies, their attendance at their churches and chapels, and their almsgiving and moral conduct, that they stared when I spoke of the love of Jesus, which brought Him down from heaven to suffer for man, and of the utter inability of man to save himself; they apparently believing that they themselves were doing the work which was to merit salvation, making the sacrifice of Christ of no effect. This, it appears to me, is the belief of a large number of nominal Christians, while a still larger number live on from day to day without giving a thought to the future, or caring whether they are to pass it in glory, or to be cast out for ever from the presence of God. I cannot bear to think that those I know should be existing in so dangerous a state without trying to make the truth known to them, and urging them to accept salvation while the day of grace lasts."

I mention this conversation, because it so exactly describes my own feelings, and the state of the greater number of people I have since met.

"How earnestly I pray that my dear father may have accepted the truth," continued Miss Kitty. "I had almost despaired of again seeing him, when a sailor, who had been wrecked in the Pacific, made his way to our island. While conversing with the poor man, who was dying, he told me that he had been on board an outward-bound ship which had picked up an English officer, who had made his escape from a French prison; and I was certain, from the name and from the description he gave me, that the officer must have been my father. The ship touched nowhere till she was wrecked on some rocks in the Southern Ocean, between the Mauritius and Australia. My father was among those who escaped. They were rescued by a South Sea whaler, which my informant quitted to join another ship, leaving him on board. Where my father was going to he could not tell, but concluded that he intended returning home. Even should he have done so, he would have been unable to hear of me, and this makes me anxious in the extreme to return home, to try and find him out."

I sympathised with Miss Kitty when she gave me this account, and told her how glad I should be to assist her in

W. H. G. Kingston

the search.

Some days after this, one of those furious gales which occasionally blow over the usually calm waters of the Pacific came on, and we unexpectedly made an island not marked in the charts, to avoid which our course was being altered, when a squall laid the ship almost on her beam-ends. Throwing off my jacket, that my arms might be perfectly unfettered, I sprang aloft with others yet further to shorten sail, when the main-topmast and the yard on which I hung were carried away. The next moment I found myself struggling amid the foaming waters. The ship flew on. To heave-to or lower a boat I knew was impossible. I gave myself up for lost: still I struck out with the instinct of self-preservation. The seas dancing wildly around circumscribed my view, and I could only just see the masts of the ship as she receded from me. Several other poor fellows I knew had been hove into the sea off the yard with me. Though dressed only in a light shirt and trousers, I was nearly exhausted. Had I retained my jacket, I believe that I should have been unable to keep myself afloat. Just then a shout reached my ears, and I saw Bill seated astride a piece of timber, not far from me. With my remaining strength I made towards it, and he, seizing me by the shirt, hauled me up, and made me fast with some rope attached to the spar.

"Glad to find you, Charley," he said. "I saw the timber, when I thought there was no hope, and got on to it. Now we must trust that the ship will come back to pick us up, or that the wind will drive us to the shore, otherwise we shall be badly off."

I thought so too; but having escaped immediate death so wonderfully, I could not help hoping that further means would be sent us for preserving our lives.

"We must trust in God," I answered. "It is a happy thing for you and me, Bill, that we are ready to go into His presence, knowing that He will receive us as loved children."

"Ah, yes, Master Charley, that's what I have been thinking," said Bill. "I knew you were on the yard, and the moment I was in the water I prayed that He would save you as well as me, and you see He has done so."

We, however, could talk but little; indeed, what we said was uttered in disjointed sentences; for the foaming sea kept tossing the log on which we sat up and down, so that we could with difficulty hold on to it. The sea-birds kept wildly screaming over our heads, while nothing could be seen around us but the foaming, troubled waters. In vain we looked out for the ship. Evening was coming on, and the gloom increased. Had it not been for the rope, we could not have maintained our hold of the log. Each time after a sea had swept over us I looked up, hoping to discover the ship, but she was nowhere visible, and even had she been near, the increased darkness would have shut her out from our sight.

Hour after hour passed by, and, faint and exhausted, I felt that I could not hold on much longer. Poor Bill seemed in even a worse condition. I could hear his voice every now and then, amid the roaring of the waters, uttering a prayer, and I joined him in my heart. At last I fell into a state of almost insensibility, and I knew not how the hours went by. Again I aroused myself, and it seemed to me that the night must have well-nigh passed by. At length the roaring sound of the waters increased: it was that of a heavy surf breaking on the shore. Daylight appeared. As the log rose to the summit of the sea, I caught sight of a rocky coast close at hand. In a few minutes more the log might be cast on it, but the danger we ran was greater than ever, for if turned over and over by the surf, we might be crushed beneath it. I cast off the lashings

W. H. G. Kingston

which bound me, holding on instead tightly to the ropes, and urging Bill to do the same. He did not appear to comprehend me. I stretched out my hand to assist him, and had just succeeded in casting loose the rope which held him, when a foaming sea took me, and I was carried forward in its embrace towards the shore. What happened to my companion I could not see, for I lost all consciousness. Confused by the roaring and hissing of the waters in my ears, it appeared to me that I was lifted up and down, and swept backwards and forwards; then I felt my hands and feet touching the shore. I struggled on. Another sea came hissing up; I dug my hands into the sand ere it passed away. Exhausted, I could exert myself no further. Had another sea overtaken me, it would have carried me helplessly off.

How long I thus remained I know not, when I felt my head lifted from the ground, and opening my eyes, I saw an old man with long hair and beard, and a benignant expression of countenance, bending over me. Taking me in his arms, he carried me some way from the water, and then again placed me on the ground, unable to proceed farther.

"How came you here, lad?" he asked, when he saw that I had sufficiently recovered to speak. "Has your ship been cast away?"

I told him how I had been carried overboard, and inquired whether my companion had been saved.

"I have seen no one," he said. "Indeed, I only just now came down to the spot to bathe, as it is one of the few places on the shore free from rocks; but I will search for him as soon as you are more recovered."

I begged him to go at once, assuring him that I already felt better.

"I must give you some food first," he said, hurrying away. He brought some fish and yams, which much restored my strength; but when I tried to get up and accompany him, I was unable to walk.

He went off with a long pole and a rope in his hand, telling me that I might rest without anxiety, as there were neither savages nor wild beasts in the island to injure me.

The warm sun soon dried my clothes, and, creeping under the shade of a rock, I fell asleep. I was awoke by hearing voices, and to my great joy, on looking up, I saw the old man, accompanied by Bill, who told me that he had clung to the timber, which had been drifted some way along the shore into a sheltered bay, where it had grounded. Thence he had scrambled over the rocks, and after searching in vain for me, had sat down in deep grief, under the idea that I had been lost.

Assisted by Bill, the old man led me to his hut, built against the side of rock at the foot of a high hill. Here he placed before us some more food.

"I cannot but welcome you, my lads," he said; "for I have spent three weary years in solitude since I was wrecked off this island, I being the sole survivor of a whole ship's company. Though I have constantly been on the look-out since then, not a sail has come near enough to see my signals—the flag I have hoisted by day, and the beacons I have kept burning at night. When I caught sight of your ship yesterday, I was in hopes that she was approaching; but when the gale came on I knew she could only do so with great peril, and was thankful when I saw her weather the island."

I was glad to know from this that the *Phoebe* had escaped.

W. H. G. Kingston

I knew by the tone of voice and manners of the old man that he was a gentleman, and, from his expressions, I guessed that he was a naval officer; but I felt a delicacy in putting questions to him, though I was anxious to learn who he was.

"We must not eat the bread of idleness," I said, when the meal was over. "Is there no work you would wish us to do?"

"All you can do now, my lads, is to lie down and rest," he answered, smiling. "When you are recovered, you will have to put up a hut for yourselves, and to cultivate some ground, as perhaps you may have to remain here as long as I have done."

"We must not go to sleep without thanking God for His great mercy to us," said Bill.

I felt rebuked. Without hesitation, I knelt down with my companion near a heap of dried grass and matting, which our host had prepared for us. He looked on, slightly astonished, but I heard him utter "Amen" at the end of my prayer.

Worn out with fatigue, we slept on till nearly daybreak the following morning.

CHAPTER TWENTY ONE

REUNION

During the first few weeks we were on the island, Bill and I built ourselves a comfortable hut, and planted a plot of ground with roots and seeds given to us by our host, several boxes of which, he said, had fortunately been washed on shore from the wreck. Great had been my astonishment to find who he was. I had been narrating my previous adventures. When I came to give him an account of Miss Kitty, I saw that he was deeply interested. He asked me question upon question. I told him of her belief that her father was still alive, and of her resolution not to marry till his return home.

"Then, dear boy, I pray more than ever that we may make our escape ere long, for I am her long missing father, Lieutenant Raglan. Misfortune has pursued me for many years, but I shall be recompensed by finding my child all you describe her."

I had not expected to find her father so old a man, but I discovered that care and anxiety had whitened his hair and furrowed his cheeks, and that he was not nearly so advanced in years as he had at first appeared.

W. H. G. Kingston

But I must be brief in my account of our stay on the island. I have not, indeed, many incidents to describe. We employed our time in fishing, searching for birds' egg and turtle eggs, and trapping birds. We also found a raft, on which we hoped to be able to push off to any vessel which might at length approach the coast.

I did not forget Miss Kitty's earnest wish that her father should be brought to a knowledge of the Truth. This encouraged me to speak to him. I then expressed my regret that we had no Bible, observing what comfort it would have afforded us, how impossible it is without it for man to know God's laws, and, consequently, to obey them.

"But surely, my young friend, men lead very moral and good lives without reading the Bible."

"They owe their knowledge of what is good and moral to the Bible alone, sir," I answered. "They get it secondhand, it is true, just as they get their knowledge of God from the Bible, although they may never look into it. Without the Bible we should still be worshipping blocks of stone, or creeping things, or the sun and stars. Without it man would never have discovered what God is, or how He desires to be worshipped."

And I then went on, as well as I was able, to speak of God's love to man, which induced Him to form His plan of salvation so exactly suited to man's wants.

"I am sure, sir," I continued, "God, who formed this beautiful world and filled it with wonders, cannot have left us without a revelation of Himself, and nowhere else but in the Bible can we find that revelation."

I happily recollected many important passages from the

Scriptures, which I quoted.

The old officer said he would think over the subject, and I left him in his hut, evidently meditating seriously on it. Day after day he introduced it, and now seemed only to take pleasure in talking of it. He was surprised to find how much Bill knew, and how clearly he could explain himself.

When people have absorbing subjects of conversation the time passes rapidly by.

I was one day seated with my new friend in the hut, when Bill rushed in, exclaiming:

"A sail in sight! a sail in sight! She is standing this way!"

We hurried to the top of the hill above the hut. A large ship was approaching the island. The wind was off shore, the sea calm. We hoisted the flag, and then hastily collecting some provisions, put them on our raft, and shoved off, determined to run every risk rather than allow her to pass us. It might have been a hard matter to get back if we failed to intercept her. We had brought a long pole with a flag at the end, to attract her attention. We exerted all our strength to paddle off. The wind was light, but in our favour. On she stood, as if intending to give the island a wide berth. We had got a considerable distance from the land. Mr Raglan moved the flag to and fro.

"We are seen, we are seen!" he exclaimed, as the ship altered her course directly for us. In a short time she hove-to; a boat was lowered and pulled up to us. We sprang into her. Questions were eagerly asked as to who we were.

"And what ship is yours?" inquired Mr Raglan.

"The *Harmony*, Captain Falconer," was the answer.

I rejoiced to hear this.

We were quickly on deck, and welcomed cordially as strangers by Captain Falconer, who did not recognise me. I lost no time, however, in making myself known, and in telling him who Mr Raglan was. I need not say how great was his satisfaction on receiving this information. He bestowed all the care and attention he possibly could on the old officer, and treated him as a son would a father.

I had not, while on the island, mentioned Captain Falconer's name to Mr Raglan, who had, therefore, no idea that he was his daughter's affianced husband.

"I consider your friend one of the finest officers of the merchant service I ever met," he said to me, one day. "A noble fellow. I can never be grateful enough for the attention he shows me."

The *Harmony* was homeward-bound.

As there was no one to do the duty of third mate, Captain Falconer gave me the berth, and much gratified me by saying how well pleased he was with the way I performed my work. The discipline of the ship was excellent, favourably contrasting with that of the *Phoebe*. Captain Falconer, following the example of her former commander, had prayers every morning and evening in his cabin, and a regular service for the men on Sundays, while he had a supply of excellent books for their instruction.

Mr Raglan was always ready to enter into conversation on religious subjects with the captain, and from the day we got on board he became a diligent reader of the Bible.

We had a quick passage to England. As soon as we reached the Thames, Captain Falconer gave me leave to go on shore, that I might visit my kind friend Mr Dear, who would, I knew, be under the belief that I had been lost.

Mr Raglan accompanied me, as I hoped that Mr Dear would be able to inform him where his daughter was residing. He had left his office when we arrived, and we therefore took a coach and drove to his residence. We were shown by the servant into the drawing-room, while she went to call her master, who was in the garden. The window was open, and we saw him walking along a path, accompanied by two ladies. He soon came into the drawing-room.

"Oh, my dear Laurel!" he exclaimed, in a voice broken by agitation, as he took my hands. "You are as one risen from the dead; we had given you up as lost. My wife will, indeed, be rejoiced to see you; and there is another lady here who will be glad to find that you are in the land of the living. Poor girl, when we heard her history we invited her to stay here, and positively refused to let her leave us."

He said this before he appeared to notice Mr Raglan. I felt somewhat embarrassed as to what to do, but I thought it best to introduce him before Mrs Dear and Miss Kitty came in.

I scarcely knew what effect the sudden announcement that his daughter was actually in his sight might have on the old officer. I resolved, in the first instance, simply to tell Mr Dear that his unknown visitor was a naval officer, who, having been shipwrecked, had come home in the *Harmony*, and then to get him to leave the room with me, that I might consult him in private. I did as I intended.

"I am very glad to see you, sir," exclaimed Mr Dear. "Pray be seated on this sofa, and excuse me: my young friend here

W. H. G. Kingston

has a word or two to say to me. Come along, Charley," and we left the room.

As soon as we were in the passage I told him who the officer was.

"Bless me!" he cried out, "that is extraordinary. I am, indeed, delighted. Will you go back and tell him that you hope his daughter will soon be with him, and then slip out again, and we will prepare Miss Kitty. I want your assistance, for I am afraid I shall be letting the truth out too soon."

I felt somewhat nervous, but I managed to break the news to my friend, and then, hurrying out. I joined Mr Dear in the garden. We found the ladies seated in an arbour at the further end. Miss Kitty, knowing me at once, uttered a cry of surprise, and ran forward with outstretched hands to meet me.

"I do not believe in ghosts," she said, "or I might have supposed that I saw yours. How did you escape?"

"What, is this Charley Laurel?" cried Mrs Dear, giving me a kind welcome, before I could answer Miss Kitty's question, which she herself repeated.

I soon told them, and this gave me an opportunity of mentioning the shipwrecked officer who had saved my life. I went on describing him, keeping my eyes fixed on Miss Kitty's face, till she exclaimed suddenly:

"Oh, Charley, tell me; is he not my father? And you say he came home with you?"

"Yes," I answered; "and he is even now waiting to see you."

"Oh, take me to him! take me to him!" she cried out.

Mr and Mrs Dear accompanied her to the house, and, leading her to the drawing-room door, left her with her long-lost parent.

I need scarcely say that Captain Falconer next day made his appearance at the house, and before he went away Mr Raglan gladly accepted him as a son-in-law.

I was glad to find that Captain Renton was again to take command of the *Phoebe*, though I should have preferred sailing with Captain Falconer. He, however, it had been arranged, in consequence of his marriage, should remain on shore for a year or two, to superintend the fitting out of Messrs. Dear and Ashe's ships.

I made two voyages in the *Phoebe*, and returned on the last as her first mate. So high a character did Captain Renton give me, that my employers promised me the command of a ship they were about to despatch to the West Indies. I passed the short time I was able to spend on shore in visiting Mr Dear and Captain and Mrs Falconer, with whom Captain Raglan, for I was glad to find he was promoted, resided.

My ship, the *Ellen*, was at length ready for sea. I felt as proud as I suppose most young officers do, when they first assume the command of a fine vessel; and as I surveyed the *Ellen*, I was satisfied that she was all I could desire.

"You need not be jealous of Falconer," said Mr Dear, who accompanied me on board. "You have now got a wife of your own, and I hope she will prove true and faithful."

Being allowed three mates, I offered the berth of third mate to Dick, who, though no navigator, was as good a seaman as I could desire to have under me.

W. H. G. Kingston

"I am obliged to you, Captain Laurel, but I am afraid I ha'n't make much of a hand of the quadrant, or managing those chronometer affairs," he answered, modestly; "though I know the stars pretty well, and can dot down what is wanted in the log."

"I won't trouble you about that," I said; "you can manage the men, which is more important. We have a rough lot, I fear."

Dick without farther ado accepted the appointment.

We were bound, in the first instance, for Barbadoes, but expected to visit other islands on our return. We had a fine run across the Atlantic. Though at first I felt a little strange, sitting in dignified solitude in my cabin, I soon got accustomed to it.

The first and second mates were sensible fellows, and learned to esteem Dick for his excellent qualities. He managed the men admirably, and got more work out of them than they could, so that all things went smoothly. He did not abuse them for swearing or coarse language, but, by bringing out his Bible, he got them to listen; and then, pointing to God's Word, asked them whether such and such things could be right in His sight. Thus by degrees they were induced to give up a habit which had become with most of them a second nature.

We had just made the north end of the Caribbean Islands soon after daylight, and were going about, to beat up to our port, as the wind was against us, when the look-out at the mast-head caught sight of a large ship which appeared to be on shore on a reef. Her sails were furled, and she was heeling over greatly. I accordingly stood on, to render her any assistance she might require. As we drew near her, we saw that she was, indeed, hard and fast, while a heavy sea broke on the reef and threatened her with destruction. Through my glass I could see that the crew were employed in lowering the yards, probably for the purpose of building a raft. I, ordering the first mate to stand off the land, lowered two boats. I took the command of one, and Dick of the other, and we pulled towards the wreck. The tide was rising, and as we got near we saw that the breakers were dashing with increasing fury against the ship. A boat crowded with people had got away on the lee side towards the land, and another, attempting to follow her example, was swamped, and we feared that all the people in her were lost. To approach on the weather side was impossible. I therefore directed Dick to follow me, and pulled away to the south'ard, hoping to get round it, as I did not believe that it extended many miles in that direction. We had, however, a long pull, and by the time we got into comparatively smooth water, having passed round the southern end of the reef, I was afraid that the fate of those on board must be sealed. When we again made out the ship, I feared that my worst anticipations had been fulfilled, for the sea broke completely over her. Her masts were gone and her upper works washed away. I got as near as I could, but could distinguish no human being on board. Her crew must either have been carried away by the sea, or made their escape in the boats, or on the raft they were forming, if, as I doubted, they had had time to finish it. Away to the westward rose a rocky island, which, from its appearance, I guessed was uninhabited, and I thought that in all probability any who had escaped would attempt to effect a landing on it. As in their hurry they were not likely to have carried either provisions or water, I determined to pull to the island, to relieve any of the people who might have reached it. As we drew near, I saw that the sea was breaking heavily on the weather shore, but I had no doubt of being able to land on the lee side. We had a long pull before us; but the men exerted themselves, and I still hoped to get back to the ship before night closed in.

W. H. G. Kingston

CHAPTER TWENTY TWO

EMILIE

On landing on the lee side of the island, I climbed to a high point near at hand, whence I could take a glance over the sea to the westward, but could discover no sign of either raft or boats, and therefore concluded that they must have been cast on the weather side; and if so, from the heavy surf which broke against it, I feared few could have scaped it.

However, with Dick and several of the men, I pushed across, carrying ropes and boat-hooks and some of the oars, to try and save any who might be clinging to the neighbouring rocks. We had not got far when I heard a voice hailing, and we caught sight of a man on the top of a rock in the centre of the island, waving to us. "Make haste! make haste!" he shouted, "or you will be too late." The stranger hurried down the rock, and we followed him.

In a few minutes we again caught sight of the sea on the east side of the island. As we were climbing over the rough ground, I saw that a reef extended some distance from the mainland, with wild rocks rising out of it above the foaming waters. Midway between them and the land was a large boat, surrounded by people, some on the reef, others clinging to the boat; while several were at that moment being carried away by the sea, which, sweeping round the rocks, beat with violence against the shattered boat. The men with frantic efforts were attempting to drag her up farther on the reef, as the only hope of saving their lives. Now one poor fellow, now another, was washed away, as the sea swept round over the reef with ever-increasing force. We were hurrying down the rocks, when I saw just below us a young lady, for I could not doubt, from her appearance, that she was such. She had been gazing at the dreadful spectacle, and apparently unable to witness it longer, she sank on the rock, pressing her hand on her eyes, to shut it out. At this moment we were joined by the stranger who had called to us.

"I caught sight of your boat coming towards the island, and was hurrying across, to entreat you to try what you could do to assist our friends," he said. "Help is at hand, Emilie; they may still be saved," he exclaimed, as he made his way to where the young lady was seated.

We got as close to the people as the sea would allow us.

"Hold on to the rope," cried Dick, securing the end round his waist. "I will swim out, and make it fast to the boat."

Fearlessly he plunged into the boiling surf, but was soon carried down far below the boat, and we hauled him back, not without great risk of his being dashed against the rocks.

"I will try it again, and start higher up the shore," he exclaimed, still undaunted.

"Let me go," cried the young stranger; "they are my friends, and I ought to run the risk."

"If I cannot manage it, you shall go the next time," answered Dick, once more plunging into the water.

He swam on directly across the boiling current, which swept him down towards the boat. He had very nearly gained a footing on the rocks, when once more he was carried down, and we hauled him back, utterly exhausted. His bravery had encouraged the rest of the men, several of whom begged that I would allow them to make the attempt.

"I said that I would go next," exclaimed the young stranger, fastening the rope round his waist, and, before I could stop him, he plunged into the water. He buffeted the waves bravely, but his strength was not equal to the undertaking. I trusted that, notwithstanding his light figure and delicate appearance, he would succeed. Every moment was precious, for one after the other the people were being carried away before our eyes, without our having the means of saving them. He had already got a footing on the reef. Just as some of the men were making their way towards him, and he had nearly got up to the boat, a sea lifted him off his feet, and he and those who were near him were swept away. My men and I hauled in the rope, but, unable to guide himself, he was dashed with violence against the rocks, and when we drew him on shore, he was almost insensible.

"Oh, my poor, poor brother!" exclaimed the young lady, who knelt down by his side. "Can nothing be done for him?"

"He will, I trust, recover," I said, "though I fear he is greatly injured. But we must make another attempt to help the poor people on the rock."

"Oh, do so, brave men!" she said, looking up with an imploring glance, her thoughts being evidently divided between her brother and those he had attempted to rescue.

Dick was preparing again to make the attempt. This time he fastened two oars under his arms, with a boat-hook lashed across them, and, supported by this simple sort of catamaran, he at length, by great exertions, reached the rocks, and secured the rope to the bow of the boat, round which the survivors were clinging. Among them were two females. Securing one of them to himself by means of a spare piece of rope, and pushing back some of the men, who were attempting to reach the shore by the rope, he began to make his way along it, resting on the oars. Every instant I dreaded to see him and his burden carried away, but he landed in safety, and we placed the almost senseless lady by the side of her friends.

We had fortunately brought a second coil of lighter rope. As I saw that Dick was exhausted I determined to go myself, and, making the rope fast round my waist, I hauled myself across, as Dick had done, though, from the difficulty I had to hold on, I judged of the danger he had gone through.

As the tide was still rising, I knew that the boat and all clinging to her must shortly be washed off the rock.

The youngest female was still safe. I secured her to my back, following Dick's example, and began hauling myself across, though every moment I expected to be washed away. As soon as she landed, she threw herself into the arms of the young lady whom we had first seen, and, from their likeness, I judged that they were sisters. I was about to return, when I saw one of the men making his way across by the rope, and that others were preparing to follow, not waiting for the assistance which the oars might afford them.

"Oh, my father, my father, is he not coming!" exclaimed the young lady I had brought on shore.

I had observed among the people on the rock a gentleman who had committed the young lady to my charge.

"I will try and save him!" I exclaimed.

At that moment loud shrieks were heard, for the sea had lifted the boat and swept her and all clinging to her off the rock. The rope still held, and my men hauled on it with right good-will. The other rope was still round my waist. I plunged into the water, and swam towards the boat. I caught sight of the gentleman just at the moment that he had been forced from his hold. In another instant he would have been carried away, when, grasping him tightly, I shouted to my men to haul me in. Almost exhausted, I was drawn on shore with the person I had rescued. Of the rest, three were thrown on the rocks, one of whom was carried away before he could make good his footing, while the remainder were swept out to sea. Besides the two we had first seen, only eight were saved. The sorrow exhibited by the ladies and the old gentleman when they saw how severely injured the young man had been in his effort to help them, made me suppose that they were relatives.

"Oh, Henri, Henri!" they murmured, bending over him.

Their accent and the last words they uttered showed me that they were French.

The young man opened his eyes and tried to smile, as if to reassure them.

"I am not so very much hurt," he answered, in a low voice.

Just then I was sure I knew the expression of his countenance; his eyes, too, glanced at my face.

"Are you not Frenchy?" I asked, "My old friend Henri de Villereine?"

"Yes, Charley. I thought I knew you," he answered. "Thank you, thank you, for what you have done!"

His companions looked at me with surprise. "I am an old schoolfellow," I said; "and I am doubly thankful that I have been the means of helping those belonging to him."

There was, however, no time for conversation or explanation beyond this. Having formed two rough litters with our oars and ropes, we placed my old schoolfellow on one and the elder lady on the other, while I and the other gentleman assisting the young ladies, we proceeded back to the boats. The provisions we had brought somewhat restored all the party.

The evening was approaching, and when I looked out for the ship I could but just distinguish her topsails above the horizon. We had a long pull before us, and I feared we should not reach her before dark, and, if so, we might have to spend the night tossed about on the stormy sea. I cheered my men, and they did their utmost. Dick had taken the seamen in his boat, and I had the passengers in mine. They were much cast down at the loss of their companions and the horrors they had gone through.

I found that the young lady who had at first landed was Henri's sister; the other I had saved was Sophie, his cousin; and the old lady and gentleman her father and mother. Thus the whole of one family had been saved, but several other passengers, men, and women, and children on board, had lost their lives.

They belonged, they told me, to the island of Saint Lucia, and were on their way to pay a visit to England, which neither of the young ladies had seen.

W. H. G. Kingston

Emilie was an intelligent, interesting-looking girl, and appeared much attached to her brother, by whose side she sat, trying to support him in as comfortable a position as could be arranged in the stern-sheets. I was, however, more struck by the gentle and sweet look of Sophie, whose features also were decidedly prettier than those of her cousin, though few girls under the circumstances could have looked attractive; and it may seem strange that I should have thought about the matter, but I had saved her life, and naturally felt an interest in her. Henri, I observed every now and then, gazed at her when he could lift up his head, but she turned away her eyes, as if unwilling to meet his, and then he sank back with a sigh.

While we pulled southward inside the reef, although the sea was somewhat heavy, it was much smoother than outside, and I feared that we might have some difficulty in getting our passengers on board. I had fortunately brought a musket and powder-flask, with some blue lights, from the ship. The sun set before we reached the southern end of the reef, and we had barely light sufficient to steer with any degree of safety round it. At length, however, I judged that I might venture to do so, and we commenced our pull out to sea. The waves broke with a loud roar on the rocks close to us, and I could distinguish the surf rising up like a white wall as we made our way to the westward. I was thankful when I saw it well over the quarter. My men exerted themselves bravely. As soon as we had got to a sufficient distance from the reef, I fired the musket and let off a blue light. There was no answer from the ship. We pulled out still farther, and in half an hour made another signal. My relief was great when, about as I judged a mile away, a blue light burst forth from the ship, showing clearly her rigging and sails as she bore down towards us.

Scarcely an expression of anxiety or alarm had escaped my

new friends, although to them the foaming seas, as we made our way over them that dark night, must have appeared truly terrible.

In a short time the ship appeared like a phantom moving over the ocean. I let off another blue light, to show our position. She hove-to, and we pulled up under her lee. As we approached, I ordered a chair to be slung, to hoist our passengers on board. The operation would be a dangerous one.

By the time we were alongside the chair was ready, with lanterns let down on either side of it. The old lady was first sent up, and then his sister and cousin entreated that Henri might go. I secured him in the chair, for he had not strength to hold on. He groaned as I did so, the boat all the time rising and falling, and there was a risk that, before he could be hoisted clear of her, she might be lifted up and strike the chair. This risk, indeed, was run by all the party. I was anxious to get the old gentleman to take his seat next, as I knew that I could with greater ease carry the lighter forms of the young ladies up in my arms. Henri was lifted on deck, and then, almost by main force, I placed Monsieur de Villereine in the chair. As soon as I saw him swinging well out of the way of the boat, taking Sophie round the waist, and telling my coxswain to follow with her cousin, I sprang up the side. It was well that I did so, for at that moment, a sea surging round almost stove in the boat and half filled her with water; but the men were ready, and, hooking on, the falls were let down, and the boat was hoisted up in time to save her being completely knocked to pieces. The party in Dick's boat took but a short time in getting on board, and she also was quickly hoisted up.

While the ship stood off the land, I went down to the cabin to attend to my passengers.

W. H. G. Kingston

I fortunately had plenty of berths. The steward set to work to get them ready, and the cook meantime was busy in preparing hot soup and arrowroot, and other things which he thought might conduce to the comfort of my unexpected guests. Having served in passenger ships, I was at no loss what to do, and the mates and I turning out our wardrobes, supplied clothing which might serve while that of the party was washed in fresh water and dried.

The night was stormy, and I was obliged constantly to be on deck, but whenever I went below, I visited poor Henri, who was suffering much. I did all I could to relieve him, and directed my steward, who was a trustworthy man, to remain by his side during my absence.

The next day the weather moderated, and I was thankful to find the rest of the party greatly recovered. They all expressed their gratitude to me for the attention I paid to their relative.

"You forget," I answered, "that he is an old schoolfellow, and that I have the greatest satisfaction possible in being of service to him."

"Ah, you must be the friend then of whom he has often spoken to us, who was so kind to him at school," observed Emilie. "We have so longed to see you, to return the kindness you showed him when he was a boy, and we hope to do so, as he said you promised to pay us a visit should you ever come to the West Indies."

I replied that I should be very glad to avail myself of the invitation he had given me, could I manage to do go, but that I feared my duty would not allow me to leave the ship on that voyage.

Henri appeared to get much better during the day. While I sat by him, he repeated the invitation his sister had given me, and entreated me to visit them, saying, his father and mother, he was sure, would be most anxious to see me.

None of the rest of the party suffered much from the exposure and alarm to which they had been subjected.

Within a week we were safely at anchor in Carlisle Bay, on the shore of which, Bridgetown, the capital of the beautiful island of Barbadoes, is situated.

CHAPTER TWENTY THREE

A HURRICANE

As soon as the anchor was dropped and the sails furled, I conveyed my passengers on shore, that I might see them comfortably lodged as soon as possible. I had offered to supply them with funds, but Monsieur de Villereine, thanking me cordially, assured me that he was well known to several merchants in Bridgetown, and that he should have no difficulty in obtaining money.

"I should be very thankful, however, if you could convey us to Saint Lucia, as we should prefer sailing in your ship to any other," he observed; "and as I am well known to your consignees, I may, perhaps, arrange the matter with them." I of course replied that I should be truly glad if this could be done, though I could not venture on my own responsibility to go there.

"Oh, but my uncle will easily manage it," observed Emilie, "so we will consider it settled. I should not like to trust my dear brother on board any other ship."

Sophie seemed inclined to speak, but hesitated: though the glance she gave me, I fancied, showed that she hoped I would not decline.

"Oh, you must come, Laurel," said Henri. "My father will, I am sure, be glad to pay any expenses of extra insurance and that sort of thing, so that the interest of your owners will not suffer."

Having seen my friends lodged at a comfortable hotel, I had to return on board to attend to my duties connected with the ship.

I lost no time in discharging my cargo, and was not sorry to find that there would be some delay before the sugar and other produce I was to receive in return would be ready.

I of course visited my friends every day, to see how poor Henri was getting on, and spent as much time with him as I could. They insisted as regularly on my remaining to dine and spend the evening. Every day that I saw the young ladies, I liked them better, and confessed to myself that I had begun to feel more than an ordinary interest for Sophie. Her eyes brightened when I entered, and her manner towards me was so gentle and so confiding, that I could not help fancying that the feelings I had for her were returned. Then I began to ask myself the question, Have I, with the precarious profession I have to depend on, without a name or family, with only one friend able to assist me, any right to attempt to win the affections of a young girl accustomed to all the luxuries of a rich planter's establishment? or is it indeed likely that her father would allow her to marry a person situated as I am? These and similar thoughts occupied my mind; and I determined, the next time I went to the house, to be very cautious in my manner, and, only paying such attentions to her and her cousin as common courtesy demanded, to devote myself rather to her uncle and aunt, or to Henri, who had now sufficiently recovered to be able to join the party in the drawing-room.

The next day, however, when I went to call on the merchants to whom the *Ellen* was consigned, they inquired whether I should have any objection to carry Monsieur de Villereine and his family to Saint Lucia.

"He has made the necessary arrangements with us, so that, if the ship is ready, you can sail the day after to-morrow."

I tried to look unconcerned, and replied that I should be very glad to do anything to accommodate them.

"We will consider the matter settled then," was the answer; "you can get ready for sea."

I own that I had had my cabins burnished up, and had procured a new dinner and tea service, while I directed the mates to get the ship in as trim order as possible. As soon as the cargo was discharged, the painters had been busy in all directions about her; while Dick, who suspected the truth, got the decks holy-stoned and scrubbed till they looked almost as white as snow.

All things were ready by the day I had been directed to sail, and early in the forenoon I went on shore to escort my passengers on board. They too were in very different guise to that when they came on board after their shipwreck. Sophie looked more sweet and lovely than ever, in the light costume which the heat of the climate required, while Emilie was cheerful and full of conversation, doing her utmost to keep up her brother's spirits. I was sorry to see less improvement in him than I had hoped. He looked pale and ill, though he declared that he had recovered from the injuries he had received when dashed against the rocks.

The weather was fine, and I did not expect to be long in running across to Saint Lucia, which is one of the nearest islands in the Caribbean Sea to Barbadoes. The wind, however, headed us soon after we got clear of the land, and a few hours afterwards it fell a dead calm, and we lay immovable on the glass-like sea. I cannot say that for my own sake I specially regretted this, though, knowing the wishes of my friends, I felt anxious to make the shortest possible passage.

I had an awning rigged, so that the ladies could spend the day on deck, where they sat busy with their needles; for, unlike the Creoles generally, they were evidently good housewives.

"As you may suppose, Captain Laurel, having lost all our things, we have plenty of work before us to make fresh ones," observed Emilie, laughing. "Though as we intended to get rigged out, as you would call it, in Paris, fortunately our loss was not so severe as it would have been on our homeward voyage. Ah, but I am wrong to talk so lightly, when I speak of that terrible event. Still, you understand, that we fancy we can make our own things better than anybody else can make them for us, and therefore you must not expect to find us sitting, like other young ladies, with our hands before us."

Sophie, however, was not so diligent as her cousin, and did not object to come to the side of the ship, and watch the strange creatures of the deep as they swam or floated by. When night came on, and the stars shone forth from the clear sky, each reflected in the deep as in a mirror, she stood with me while I told her their names. I was scarcely aware how time had passed by, when I heard Monsieur de Villereine's voice summoning his niece, and telling her that it was time for her to retire to her cabin.

I was never addicted to whistling for a wind, and certainly

should not have done so on that occasion. A breeze, however, came at last, and the *Ellen* gliding swiftly over the calm sea, we came in sight of that most beautiful and picturesque island of Saint Lucia.

Two lofty heights of a sugar-loaf form, shooting up from the sea, and feathered from base to summit with the richest foliage, were the first objects which attracted our attention. Beyond these rose a range of mountains, running north and south through the island, and broken into the most fantastic shapes. As we sailed along the shore, having the mountains still as the background, here and there appeared the most lovely little caves and bays, fringed with luxuriant cane-fields, and enlivened by the neatly laid-out mansions of the planters; while numerous fishing and passage boats, with their long light masts and lateen sails, were gliding over the calm waters.

"I used to tell you, Laurel, that our island was one of the most beautiful in the world—don't you think so?" said Henri, as, while standing near his sister and cousin, I was watching the shore, and every now and then addressing them.

"Indeed it is. I am not surprised that you are so fond of it, and, could I leave the sea, I should be content to spend my days there," I answered, speaking as I felt.

"Oh, do," exclaimed Henri. "Come and turn planter; we can give you plenty of occupation, and my health as been so bad lately, that I should be glad if you could take my place."

"I am afraid that, having lived so little on shore, I should make but a poor farmer," I answered, laughing.

Sophie looked up at me, and remarked: "The difficulties to be overcome are not very great, I suspect, and I am sure you would soon learn all that is necessary."

"The proposal is indeed a tempting one," I answered; "and yet I love the sea, and should be sorry to abandon it."

"Oh, you can take an occasional trip to England," observed Henri. "Have a ship of your own, and just make a voyage when you get tired of the shore."

Our conversation was interrupted by a shift of wind, which compelled me to issue orders for trimming sails.

The steward then announced luncheon, and I remained some time on deck after my passengers had gone below.

I had observed Dick, who did not often trouble himself about scenery, watching the coast with more than usual interest.

"Do you know, captain," he said, coming up to me, "I have a notion that I have seen this island before. The look of the coast is very like that we sailed along when I was aboard the *Laurel*, before I picked you up. I shall be able to tell better when we come off the harbour, for then I think I should be sure to know the place again. It will be strange if it should turn out that I am right in my idea, and if so, I would advise you to make inquiries, and learn if any of the families on shore about that time lost a little boy in the way you were lost. Maybe, as the newspapers say, you will hear of something to your advantage; and if you don't, why you won't be worse off than you are now, and you may be very sure that as long as Dick Driver lives, you have got a friend who will stick to you, blow high or blow low."

"I am sure you will, Dick," I answered. "Though perhaps, as many years have passed by since you were last on these seas, you may be mistaken as to the island."

Yet, although I said this, I could not help allowing strange hopes and fears to agitate my bosom. I might discover my parents, or they might be dead, and their successors might be unwilling to acknowledge a stranger coming among them. I could scarcely calm myself sufficiently to go into the cabin. I determined, however, to say nothing about Dick's remarks, but to try and overcome all the hopes which I found rising within me. I apologised for being late to luncheon, on the plea of being detained on deck by duty, and did my best to perform the honours of the table and try to converse in my usual manner. The ladies were eager to know when I thought we should get in.

"The wind is so light that I do not expect to enter the harbour till to-morrow morning," I replied. "I cannot pretend to regret this, as I know my stay will be very short, and it will defer the time when I must bid you farewell."

Sophie looked up at me, and a shade of sadness passed over her sweet countenance. I could not be mistaken. I interpreted her feelings by my own, and just then I would have given a great deal to have had a proper excuse for remaining at Saint Lucia.

Night came on, and the *Ellen* floated calmly on the moonlit sea. Emilie had insisted on Henri going below, afraid of his being exposed to the night-air: indeed, the trying cough from which he suffered showed how necessary it was that all care should be taken of him.

Sophie still lingered on deck. I invited her to come to the side and watch the moonbeams playing on the waters.

"I know what sailors have to go through," she observed, "but yet I fancy the enjoyments of a night like this must almost recompense them for the tempest and rough seas they have to endure."

"We get so well accustomed to both one and the other. Though acknowledging the beauty of the ocean under all its various phases, whether sleeping as now under the beams of the pale moon, or glowing in the rays of the ruddy sun, we value them less, I fear, than those who only occasionally venture on the world of waters," I remarked.

"Oh, but I am sure I could never look with indifference on such a scene as this," said Sophie, "and should be content to make voyage after voyage to witness it."

However, I do not feel disposed to say what else we talked about. I was young, and said what I certainly did not intend to say. I told Sophie that I loved her, and would never marry any one else. She did not withdraw her hand, and, whispering that I had made her very happy, promised that she would be faithful to me, and that she did not suppose her father and mother would object to me, especially as I was the friend of her cousin.

The time flew by faster than I supposed, as we thus stood talking; Dick, who had charge of the deck, keeping at a judicious distance.

Suddenly the light on the water disappeared, a cloud had obscured the moon; again the light shone forth, and again was shut out; still no wind filled our sails. I knew, however, that it might come ere long. Sophie still lingered by my side. Hitherto the ocean had slept in silence. Suddenly a rushing murmuring sound fell on my ear.

"Hands aloft, and shorten sail!" I shouted. There was not a moment to be lost.

W. H. G. Kingston

"Go below, I entreat you," I said, leading Sophie to the companion-hatch.

"Oh, what is going to happen?" she asked, in an anxious tone.

"A hurricane is, I fear, upon us," I answered, "and you will be safer below."

She no longer hesitated, and her father, aroused by my voice, happily came to assist her down.

"Turn the hands up!" I shouted to Dick, who hurried forward to rouse up the watch below.

In less than a minute the other mates and the rest of the crew were on deck. Courses were hauled up, topgallant sheets were let fly, topsails lowered. The crew had sprung aloft. The fore-topsail was hauled, but before the men were off the yards, the hurricane was down upon us. Over the ship heeled. In an instant the topgallantsails were blown to ribbons.

"Down, for your lives, down!" I shouted. No human power could have handled the canvas now, with wild roars lashing furiously in the wind. The main and mizen-topsails were blown out of the bolt-ropes, and soon with innumerable coils encircled the yards. The ship, relieved of the pressure of the sails, righted. Happily the wind was off the land, or in a few minutes she would have been driven on shore. Still there was the danger of it shifting; I therefore put the helm up, and ran off before the wind. Every instant the sea rose, and as she got farther and farther from the land, she began to pitch and tumble wildly about. Dick and several hands, going aloft with axes, at length cleared the topgallant yards, and we got them down on deck, and struck the gallant masts. Getting the main-topsail set, a lull occurring, I was able to heave her to.

Not till then could I venture to leave the deck. On entering the cabin, I found my passengers clinging to the sofas. By the light which swung to and fro in the centre, I saw that they all looked pale and alarmed, expecting again to have to encounter the fearful dangers from which they had lately escaped. I did my best to reassure them, by expressing my hopes that the hurricane would soon cease, and that, God protecting us, we might be able to enter port.

"Oh, then I have no fear," exclaimed Sophie; and raising her head, she did her best to impart the same confidence she felt to her companions.

Not knowing, however, what might occur, I was compelled again to return quickly to the deck. The gale howled and whistled through the rigging, the waves roared, and the sea, as it rose in wild billows around, every now and then broke on board, threatening to sweep our decks clear of all upon them. The lightning, darting from the clouds in vivid flashes, played around our masts. At any instant the electric fluid might, I knew full well, come hissing down on deck, and set the ship on fire. Should also the wind shift, we should lose more of our sails, and might be driven before daylight helplessly on shore.

It was a very anxious time; for I felt that I had not only the ship to look after, but her whom I loved more than my life, and those dear to her, under my charge.

Still the confidence in God's protecting care which has cheered me through life supported me on that trying occasion. I knew too that it was enjoyed by my friends; for, from the conversations I had had with them, I had discovered that they possessed the same faith as I did, and though, from living among those who differed from them, they did not speak in public on religious subjects, they made the precepts of the Bible the rule of their lives.

CHAPTER TWENTY FOUR

A HAPPY DISCOVERY

Morning broke at length. How different was the appearance of the ocean to that it had presented the previous day! The dark-green foam-topped waves danced up wildly, the sky was of a murky hue, the wind roared and whistled as loudly as before, and the ship, instead of gliding on with calm dignity, tumbled and tossed as if she was a mere cock-boat.

Sophie begged to come on deck. I assisted her up. Scarcely had she appeared, when there came a break in the clouds to the eastward, and the sun shone forth. "A good omen!" she exclaimed.

"We may take it as such," I answered; "and I trust that before long the hurricane will cease, and He who holds the waters in His hands will save us from further danger."

The wind ceased almost as suddenly as it had arisen, the sea went down, and in a few hours we were able to clear the yards and bend fresh sails. Once more the ship was standing for the land.

My first mate had frequently been at Saint Lucia, and he acting as pilot, soon after daylight the next morning we

W. H. G. Kingston

entered the harbour.

The ship of necessity must I found be detained some days, as the main-topmast was badly sprung, while she had received other damages in the gale. As these could be repaired under the superintendence of my first mate, I escorted my passengers on shore.

Monsieur de Villereine had begged me to come to his house, which was situated about a mile from the town, but I felt compelled to accept Henri's invitation to accompany him and his sister to his father's house, a short distance farther off on the side of the mountain; and more so, as from his weak state, he required my assistance in getting in and out of the carriage. Poor fellow! my heart grieved for him, as it seemed to me, though he had no apprehension of danger, that he was only returning home to die.

I had asked Sophie whether she had mentioned our engagement to her father and mother.

"I will do so immediately we get home," she answered; "it would be better than saying anything at present."

Monsieur de Villereine's house stood on elevated ground, with extensive sugar plantations below it. It was of a considerable size, surrounded by a broad verandah. The handsome appearance of the interior, and the numerous domestic slaves, gave me an idea of the wealth of the owners. I could not help asking myself, "Will Sophie be content to exchange all this luxury for the limited income and small house which I should alone have the power of offering her?" I had but one moment to speak to her alone. She seemed to divine my thoughts.

"I do not value all these things," she said, pressing my hand;

"and I trust that my brothers will live to occupy this house."

She had already told me of her two brothers, who were away on the other side of the island.

After resting some time, we continued our journey to the house of Henri's father and mother. A messenger had been sent on to warn them of our coming.

I was much pleased with the elder Monsieur de Villereine and his wife. They received me in the most kind and cordial way, but I saw how deeply they were grieved at the altered appearance of poor Henri, and that they were evidently far more alarmed than Emilie had been, who had constantly watched him. Their house was even handsomer than that of Sophie's father, though built in the same style. It commanded a beautiful view of the town and harbour and the blue sea beyond it, while on every side below stretched out the numerous sugar plantations; while here and there were seen the whitewashed houses of the inhabitants, with their gaily-painted verandahs and window blinds.

Though her manner was gentle and kind in the extreme, Madame de Villereine's countenance wore an expression of sadness which seemed habitual to it. I concluded, however, that this arose very much from her anxiety about the health of her only son. Emilie tried to cheer up her parents by assuring them that Henri was better than he had been, and she hoped that before long they should be able to carry out their project of visiting England.

"Though not our native air, it is yours, you know, mamma, and I am sure it will effectually restore his health."

Madame de Villereine shook her head.

"I had thought so," she observed; "but I see a great change in him for the worse, and I fear he is sinking under the same complaint which carried off my dear sister."

In the course of conversation she happened to mention that the sister of whom she spoke was a Mrs Raglan. I was struck by the name, and inquired who she had married.

"An officer in the navy," she answered; "but he was ordered to the East Indies, and soon afterwards she died, leaving a little girl. We received notice of her death, but the island being at the time in the possession of France, and war raging, we were never able to ascertain what became of the child."

Emilie I saw seemed anxious when her mother began to speak on this subject, and endeavoured, without appearing to do so, to change the conversation. Soon afterwards her mother seemed much affected, and left the room.

"I must ask you," said Emilie, "not again to allude to the subject, as it recalls many painful associations."

"I will do as you wish," I answered, "but I feel sure that I am well acquainted with the niece she spoke of;" and I then told her all I knew of Kitty Raglan, my meeting with her father, and her marriage with my old friend Captain Falconer.

She expressed her pleasure at what I had told her, adding, "It will, I am sure, give great joy to mother, for she has always grieved at having lost all traces of my cousin, though she has still greater grief of her own."

Just then Madame de Villereine returned, and Emilie cautiously prepared her for the interesting information I had to give.

"This is indeed joyful news," she exclaimed, when I had told her of her niece's happy marriage with Captain Falconer; when suddenly she stopped and sighed, and the sad expression which her countenance usually wore stole over it.

"Monsieur de Villereine will to-day drive you over to see his brother and his wife and daughter, and you must give them the account you have given me. They will be greatly interested; and oh, how I wish we could persuade Captain Falconer to come over and pay us a visit!"

A carriage shortly afterwards came to the door, and I accompanied my new friend—Emilie wishing to remain with Henri. Monsieur de Villereine, who had observed our approach, received as at the door. He welcomed me with marked politeness, but it struck me that his manner was much more stiff and formal than it had before been. He conducted us to the drawing-room, where I hoped to see Sophie, but her mother alone was there. I was struck also by the change of manner of the old lady, though she was as studiously polite and courteous as her husband. Having begged me to be seated, and made various common-place inquiries, he led his brother out of the room, while the old lady continued the conversation in the same formal strain. When I inquired for Sophie, expressing my hope that she had recovered from the fatigues of the voyage, she answered that her daughter was in her room, and that she did not think she would be able to leave it that morning.

After some time, when it seemed to me that we had exhausted all subjects of conversation, and my tongue had begun in a most uncomfortable way to cling to my mouth, for I somehow or other had forgotten all about Mrs Falconer, and that I had undertaken to narrate her history to her uncle and aunt, I was in truth thinking only of Sophie and myself, the two brothers returned and the old lady retired. They then

W. H. G. Kingston

sat down opposite to me, and I could not help feeling, by the expression of their countenances and their manner, that something not over agreeable was coming. Monsieur de Villereine looked at his brother and then at me, and hummed and hawed several times, as if he did not like to begin what he had to say. At last he mustered courage.

"My dear Captain Laurel," he began, "I am sure that as a sailor you like open and frank dealing. Now, I need not tell you how much we esteem you, and how grateful we are for the inestimable service you have rendered us, and for your kindness and attention while we were on board your ship; but you must acknowledge that I ought not as a father to allow these considerations to bias me when my daughter's future prospects are concerned. Now you will understand, my brother and I had agreed that she should marry her cousin Henri, although she herself is not aware of this arrangement. My astonishment was nevertheless very great when she told me that you had offered her your hand, and that she, young and inexperienced as she is, had, without consulting me, ventured to accept you. Such a thing, my dear sir, is against all precedent. The whole of society would be subverted, and all parental authority destroyed, were I as a father to allow what you do me the honour of proposing to take place. I am, I repeat, deeply grateful to you for the inestimable service you have rendered me, but I must ask you to be generous, and not insist on my giving you the reward you demand."

"My dear sir," I exclaimed, "I do not ask for your daughter's hand as a reward for anything I have done, though I esteem it the highest prize I could win. The service you are pleased to say I have rendered you, I should equally have given to any fellow-creature, and I therefore ask your daughter's hand as a free gift. I love her devotedly, and she has consented, with your permission, to be mine."

"My permission I cannot give, Captain Laurel," exclaimed the old gentleman, growing more and more agitated. "I desire to reward you to the utmost of my power, and you have my sincere and hearty gratitude; but more I cannot and will not offer. I regret deeply to say this, and I am grieved—greatly grieved. My brother knows my determination, and I am sure that you will agree that it is better I should express it at once."

In vain I attempted to plead my cause. I entreated to see Sophie, but her father replied that that would only be painful and useless; and at length the elder Monsieur de Villereine observing that his carriage was ready, I took the hint, and, feeling as if I was walking in a dream, I got into it. I felt dreadfully cast down. It seemed to me that Sophie was lost to me for ever, and I might not again have an opportunity of seeing her.

"I have some few commissions to perform in the town," said my friend, "and we will drive there. But notwithstanding what has occurred, I must insist on your coming back with me to see Henri: he and his sister will afford you all the consolation they can. But my brother is very determined, and I know him so well that I cannot tell you to keep up your hopes. It would be wiser for you to abandon them altogether."

We reached the town, and when we got there I was much inclined to go on board the ship and remain: but Monsieur de Villereine pressed me so earnestly to return, that, for the sake of Henri, I agreed to do so. As, however, I wished to go on board for a short time, he undertook to wait for me. Taking a boat from the shore, I pulled out to the *Ellen*. I had not been long on board before Dick asked me to step into the cabin, as he had something of interest to communicate to me.

W. H. G. Kingston

"Well, Captain Laurel," he said, as soon as we were seated, "I went on shore yesterday evening and walked up the town, and I am as sure as I am alive that this is the very place where you came from. As I walked up the street, I came to the very spot where the black woman handed you to me when you were a little chap scarcely higher than my knee—I could swear to it in any court of justice, if it were necessary—and, as I think I have told you, I have always carried about me the very coral you had on at the time; and now I would advise you to lose no time in making inquiries about the matter among your friends."

So wretched did I feel, that I was very little disposed to do this, and had I not promised to rejoin Monsieur de Villereine, I think that I should have remained on board, to get ready for sailing as fast as possible. I however told Dick that I would do as he recommended.

I found Monsieur de Villereine waiting on the quay for me. As soon as we had got clear of the town, I began to speak to him on the subject. As I went on, I was surprised at the extraordinary agitation he exhibited.

"Do I understand from you, my dear sir, that you yourself were carried away from this island when about four years of age?" he asked, pulling up his horse, as if he felt unable to guide the animal, and gazing at me earnestly.

"One of my mates, who has acted the part of a father to me, has assured me so," I answered, "though I myself have a very indistinct recollection even of events which occurred much after that."

"The ways of heaven are indeed mysterious," exclaimed Monsieur de Villereine. "At the time you mention, my second son, two years younger than Henri, while in charge of a black nurse, was lost to us. The poor woman was wounded by a chance shot during an attack from an English squadron, and she died shortly afterwards without being able to give any account of what had become of the child, though we had hopes that he had been carried on board one of the men-of-war. As, however, two of them were afterwards lost, we abandoned all expectation of ever again seeing our son. I must not raise your hopes too high, nor my own, and yet when I look at your features, and think of what my son might have been, I cannot but believe that you are indeed my lost boy. His name, too, was Charles, which may be a remarkable coincidence. You tell me that that name was given you on board the ship."

As may be supposed, my heart beat violently as Monsieur de Villereine said this; yet I could not help trusting that he was indeed my father.

That he might himself make inquiries of Dick, I offered to send on board at once for my mate. We accordingly drove back into the town. Dick soon arrived at the hotel, where we remained for him. Monsieur de Villereine cross-questioned him narrowly, and on his producing the coral I spoke of, any doubts he might have entertained vanished.

"My dear boy," he exclaimed, embracing me, "you are indeed my long-lost son. Your recovery will, I trust, be the means of preserving your poor mother's life, for she has, I fear, a great grief in store for her; for, although she hoped for the best, I cannot but see that your poor brother Henri's days are numbered."

I need not repeat what more my father said. Taking Dick in the carriage, we drove rapidly home. My father hurried in first to prepare my mother, and in a few minutes I had the happiness of being clasped in her arms, and receiving the affectionate kisses of my sister Emilie and the warm congratulations of poor Henri.

"I always loved you as a brother," he exclaimed; "and now I am indeed delighted to find that you are so in reality."

I was scarcely aware how quickly the time had gone by, when carriage wheels were heard approaching the house.

"I sent off a note to your uncle and aunt," said Emilie to me, "as I was sure they would be glad to hear the news, and here they are."

They entered the room directly afterwards, followed by Sophie. The formal manner my uncle had assumed had vanished. After he and my aunt had cordially welcomed me, the whole party disappeared from the room with the exception of Sophie.

"Papa has withdrawn his objection," she whispered; "and I told him I would never marry any one but you."

I must bring my yarn to a conclusion.

My first mate was so trustworthy a man, that I felt justified in sending the *Ellen* back to Barbadoes under his charge to receive her cargo.

Poor Henri entreated that I would not delay my marriage, and Sophie having no objections, in the course of a few weeks we were united. My brother's death, which all expected, took place, to our great grief, a short time afterwards.

I was thankful to find that the consignees of the *Ellen* consented to allow my mate to take her home. On her next voyage my parents and sister, as well as my uncle and aunt, agreed to accompany me to England, leaving my brothers-in-law in charge of their two estates.

We had a prosperous passage, and having been invited by Mr and Mrs Dear to pay them a visit, we on our arrival repaired to their house, where Captain and Mrs Falconer had come to receive us; and I had the happiness of introducing my old friend, and now my cousin Kitty, to her aunt and to the rest of her relations.

THE END

W. H. G. Kingston

ABOUT THE AUTHOR

William Henry Giles Kingston (1814 - 1880), writer of tales for boys, born in London, but spent much of his youth in Oporto, where his father was a merchant.

His first book, The Circassian Chief, appeared in 1844. His first book for boys, Peter the Whaler, was published in 1851, and had such success that he retired from business and devoted himself entirely to the production of this kind of literature, in which his popularity was deservedly great; and during 30 years he wrote upwards of 130 tales, including The Three Midshipmen (1862), The Three Lieutenants (1874), The Three Commanders (1875), The Three Admirals (1877), Digby Heathcote, etc.

He also conducted various papers, including The Colonist, and Colonial Magazine and East India Review. He was also interested in emigration, volunteering, and various philanthropic schemes. For services in negotiating a commercial treaty with Portugal he received a Portuguese knighthood, and for his literary labours a Government pension.

Choose from Thousands of 1stWorldLibrary Classics By

A. M. Barnard
Ada Leverson
Adolphus William Ward
Aesop
Agatha Christie
Alexander Aaronsohn
Alexander Kielland
Alexandre Dumas
Alfred Gatty
Alfred Ollivant
Alice Duer Miller
Alice Turner Curtis
Alice Dunbar
Allen Chapman
Alleyne Ireland
Ambrose Bierce
Amelia E. Barr
Amory H. Bradford
Andrew Lang
Andrew McFarland Davis
Andy Adams
Angela Brazil
Anna Alice Chapin
Anna Sewell
Annie Besant
Annie Hamilton Donnell
Annie Payson Call
Annie Roe Carr
Annonaymous
Anton Chekhov
Archibald Lee Fletcher
Arnold Bennett
Arthur C. Benson
Arthur Conan Doyle
Arthur M. Winfield
Arthur Ransome
Arthur Schnitzler
Arthur Train
Atticus
B.H. Baden-Powell
B. M. Bower
B. C. Chatterjee
Baroness Emmuska Orczy
Baroness Orczy
Basil King
Bayard Taylor
Ben Macomber
Bertha Muzzy Bower
Bjornstjerne Bjornson

Booth Tarkington
Boyd Cable
Bram Stoker
C. Collodi
C. E. Orr
C. M. Ingleby
Carolyn Wells
Catherine Parr Traill
Charles A. Eastman
Charles Amory Beach
Charles Dickens
Charles Dudley Warner
Charles Farrar Browne
Charles Ives
Charles Kingsley
Charles Klein
Charles Hanson Towne
Charles Lathrop Pack
Charles Romyn Dake
Charles Whibley
Charles Willing Beale
Charlotte M. Braeme
Charlotte M. Yonge
Charlotte Perkins Stetson
Clair W. Hayes
Clarence Day Jr.
Clarence E. Mulford
Clemence Housman
Confucius
Coningsby Dawson
Cornelis DeWitt Wilcox
Cyril Burleigh
D. H. Lawrence
Daniel Defoe
David Garnett
Dinah Craik
Don Carlos Janes
Donald Keyhoe
Dorothy Kilner
Dougan Clark
Douglas Fairbanks
E. Nesbit
E. P. Roe
E. Phillips Oppenheim
E. S. Brooks
Earl Barnes
Edgar Rice Burroughs
Edith Van Dyne
Edith Wharton

Edward Everett Hale
Edward J. O'Biren
Edward S. Ellis
Edwin L. Arnold
Eleanor Atkins
Eleanor Hallowell Abbott
Eliot Gregory
Elizabeth Gaskell
Elizabeth McCracken
Elizabeth Von Arnim
Ellem Key
Emerson Hough
Emilie F. Carlen
Emily Bronte
Emily Dickinson
Enid Bagnold
Enilor Macartney Lane
Erasmus W. Jones
Ernie Howard Pie
Ethel May Dell
Ethel Turner
Ethel Watts Mumford
Eugene Sue
Eugenie Foa
Eugene Wood
Eustace Hale Ball
Evelyn Everett-green
Everard Cotes
F. H. Cheley
F. J. Cross
F. Marion Crawford
Fannie E. Newberry
Federick Austin Ogg
Ferdinand Ossendowski
Fergus Hume
Florence A. Kilpatrick
Fremont B. Deering
Francis Bacon
Francis Darwin
Frances Hodgson Burnett
Frances Parkinson Keyes
Frank Gee Patchin
Frank Harris
Frank Jewett Mather
Frank L. Packard
Frank V. Webster
Frederic Stewart Isham
Frederick Trevor Hill
Frederick Winslow Taylor

Friedrich Kerst
Friedrich Nietzsche
Fyodor Dostoyevsky
G.A. Henty
G.K. Chesterton
Gabrielle E. Jackson
Garrett P. Serviss
Gaston Leroux
George A. Warren
George Ade
Geroge Bernard Shaw
George Cary Eggleston
George Durston
George Ebers
George Eliot
George Gissing
George MacDonald
George Meredith
George Orwell
George Sylvester Viereck
George Tucker
George W. Cable
George Wharton James
Gertrude Atherton
Gordon Casserly
Grace E. King
Grace Gallatin
Grace Greenwood
Grant Allen
Guillermo A. Sherwell
Gulielma Zollinger
Gustav Flaubert
H. A. Cody
H. B. Irving
H.C. Bailey
H. G. Wells
H. H. Munro
H. Irving Hancock
H. R. Naylor
H. Rider Haggard
H. W. C. Davis
Haldeman Julius
Hall Caine
Hamilton Wright Mabie
Hans Christian Andersen
Harold Avery
Harold McGrath
Harriet Beecher Stowe
Harry Castlemon
Harry Coghill
Harry Houidini

Hayden Carruth
Helent Hunt Jackson
Helen Nicolay
Hendrik Conscience
Hendy David Thoreau
Henri Barbusse
Henrik Ibsen
Henry Adams
Henry Ford
Henry Frost
Henry James
Henry Jones Ford
Henry Seton Merriman
Henry W Longfellow
Herbert A. Giles
Herbert Carter
Herbert N. Casson
Herman Hesse
Hildegard G. Frey
Homer
Honore De Balzac
Horace B. Day
Horace Walpole
Horatio Alger Jr.
Howard Pyle
Howard R. Garis
Hugh Lofting
Hugh Walpole
Humphry Ward
Ian Maclaren
Inez Haynes Gillmore
Irving Bacheller
Isabel Cecilia Williams
Isabel Hornibrook
Israel Abrahams
Ivan Turgenev
J.G.Austin
J. Henri Fabre
J. M. Barrie
J. M. Walsh
J. Macdonald Oxley
J. R. Miller
J. S. Fletcher
J. S. Knowles
J. Storer Clouston
J. W. Duffield
Jack London
Jacob Abbott
James Allen
James Andrews
James Baldwin

James Branch Cabell
James DeMille
James Joyce
James Lane Allen
James Lane Allen
James Oliver Curwood
James Oppenheim
James Otis
James R. Driscoll
Jane Abbott
Jane Austen
Jane L. Stewart
Janet Aldridge
Jens Peter Jacobsen
Jerome K. Jerome
Jessie Graham Flower
John Buchan
John Burroughs
John Cournos
John F. Kennedy
John Gay
John Glasworthy
John Habberton
John Joy Bell
John Kendrick Bangs
John Milton
John Philip Sousa
John Taintor Foote
Jonas Lauritz Idemil Lie
Jonathan Swift
Joseph A. Altsheler
Joseph Carey
Joseph Conrad
Joseph E. Badger Jr
Joseph Hergesheimer
Joseph Jacobs
Jules Vernes
Julian Hawthrone
Julie A Lippmann
Justin Huntly McCarthy
Kakuzo Okakura
Karle Wilson Baker
Kate Chopin
Kenneth Grahame
Kenneth McGaffey
Kate Langley Bosher
Kate Langley Bosher
Katherine Cecil Thurston
Katherine Stokes
L. A. Abbot
L. T. Meade

L. Frank Baum
Latta Griswold
Laura Dent Crane
Laura Lee Hope
Laurence Housman
Lawrence Beasley
Leo Tolstoy
Leonid Andreyev
Lewis Carroll
Lewis Sperry Chafer
Lilian Bell
Lloyd Osbourne
Louis Hughes
Louis Joseph Vance
Louis Tracy
Louisa May Alcott
Lucy Fitch Perkins
Lucy Maud Montgomery
Luther Benson
Lydia Miller Middleton
Lyndon Orr
M. Corvus
M. H. Adams
Margaret E. Sangster
Margret Howth
Margaret Vandercook
Margaret W. Hungerford
Margret Penrose
Maria Edgeworth
Maria Thompson Daviess
Mariano Azuela
Marion Polk Angellotti
Mark Overton
Mark Twain
Mary Austin
Mary Catherine Crowley
Mary Cole
Mary Hastings Bradley
Mary Roberts Rinehart
Mary Rowlandson
M. Wollstonecraft Shelley
Maud Lindsay
Max Beerbohm
Myra Kelly
Nathaniel Hawthrone
Nicolo Machiavelli
O. F. Walton
Oscar Wilde

Owen Johnson
P.G. Wodehouse
Paul and Mabel Thorne
Paul G. Tomlinson
Paul Severing
Percy Brebner
Percy Keese Fitzhugh
Peter B. Kyne
Plato
Quincy Allen
R. Derby Holmes
R. L. Stevenson
R. S. Ball
Rabindranath Tagore
Rahul Alvares
Ralph Bonehill
Ralph Henry Barbour
Ralph Victor
Ralph Waldo Emmerson
Rene Descartes
Ray Cummings
Rex Beach
Rex E. Beach
Richard Harding Davis
Richard Jefferies
Richard Le Gallienne
Robert Barr
Robert Frost
Robert Gordon Anderson
Robert L. Drake
Robert Lansing
Robert Lynd
Robert Michael Ballantyne
Robert W. Chambers
Rosa Nouchette Carey
Rudyard Kipling
Saint Augustine
Samuel B. Allison
Samuel Hopkins Adams
Sarah Bernhardt
Sarah C. Hallowell
Selma Lagerlof
Sherwood Anderson
Sigmund Freud
Standish O'Grady
Stanley Weyman
Stella Benson
Stella M. Francis

Stephen Crane
Stewart Edward White
Stijn Streuvels
Swami Abhedananda
Swami Parmananda
T. S. Ackland
T. S. Arthur
The Princess Der Ling
Thomas A. Janvier
Thomas A Kempis
Thomas Anderton
Thomas Bailey Aldrich
Thomas Bulfinch
Thomas De Quincey
Thomas Dixon
Thomas H. Huxley
Thomas Hardy
Thomas More
Thornton W. Burgess
U. S. Grant
Upton Sinclair
Valentine Williams
Various Authors
Vaughan Kester
Victor Appleton
Victor G. Durham
Victoria Cross
Virginia Woolf
Wadsworth Camp
Walter Camp
Walter Scott
Washington Irving
Wilbur Lawton
Wilkie Collins
Willa Cather
Willard F. Baker
William Dean Howells
William le Queux
W. Makepeace Thackeray
William W. Walter
William Shakespeare
Winston Churchill
Yei Theodora Ozaki
Yogi Ramacharaka
Young E. Allison
Zane Grey